HOW TO DRAW SEXY, RETRO
SPACE GIRLS!

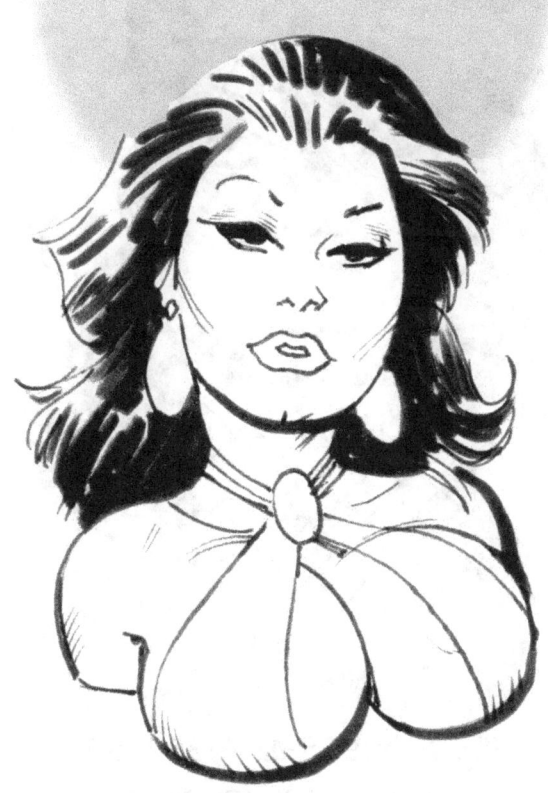

by MIKE HOFFMAN

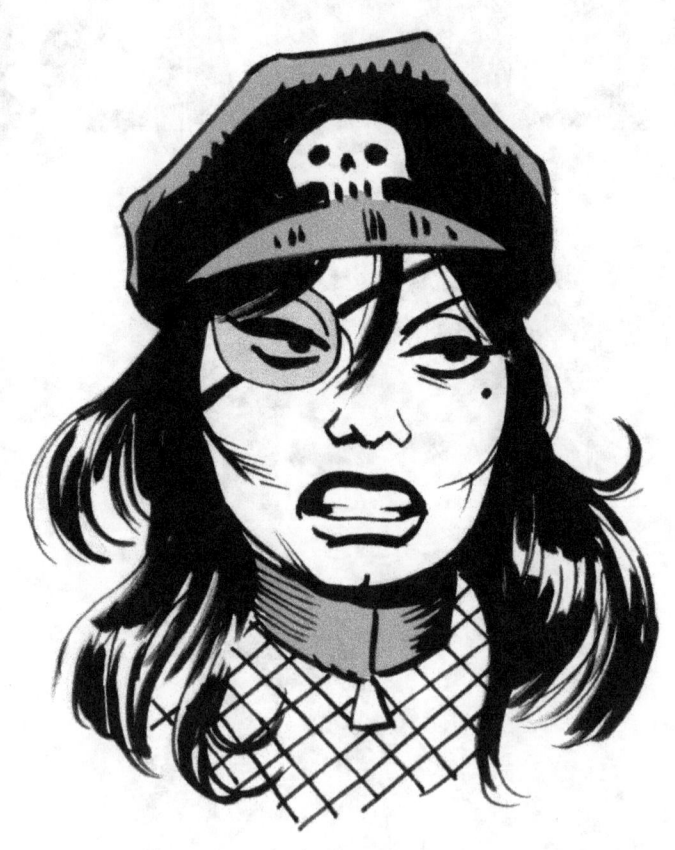

ISBN-13:978-1974362189
ISBN-10:1974362183

Second Printing

Materials

All the drawings in this book were made with the various **marker-pens** shown below!

Real art brushes and **dip pens** are really **better**, but they ain't **faster**!

Besides, you can always **graduate** to those later...

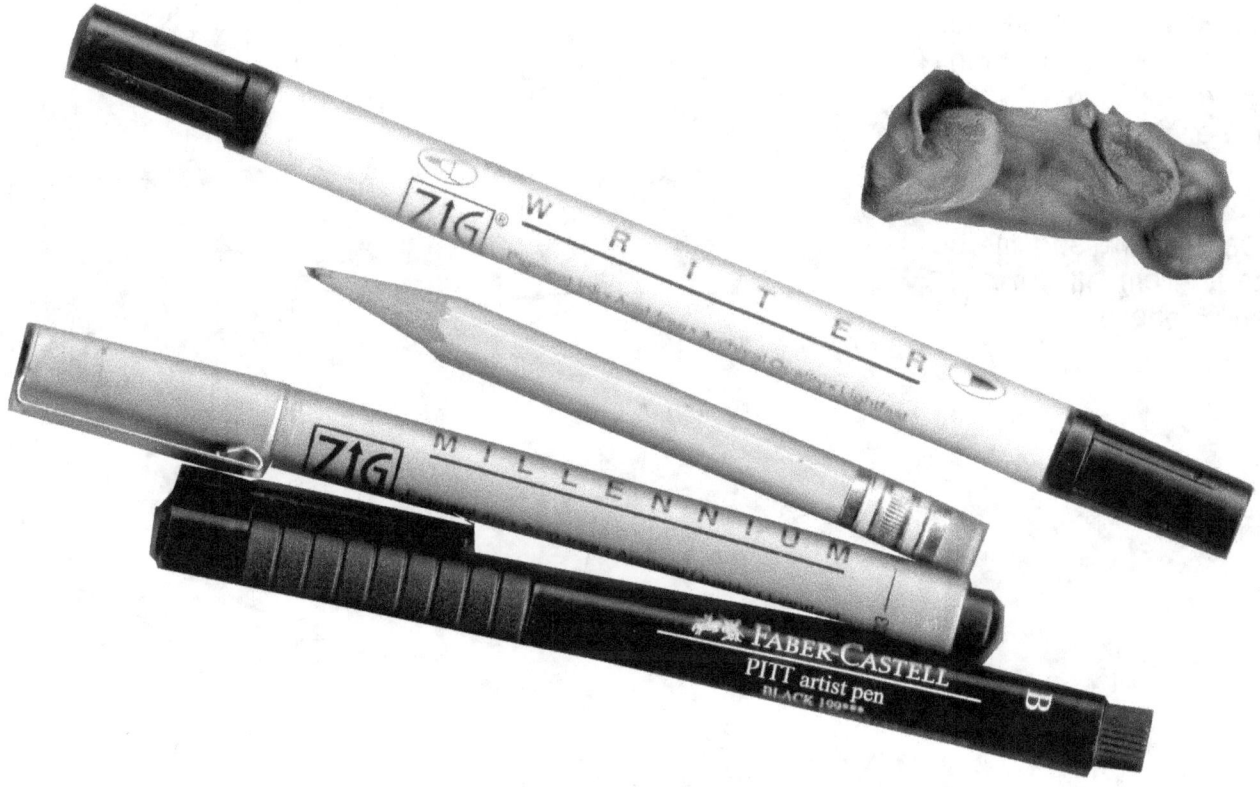

The **Zig Millennium** pen is a **size 03**, and we used it for the **finest lines**!

Also, a **kneaded eraser** is essential!

The Playing Card Trick...

Everybody knows what a standard **Playing Card** looks like.

You're not supposed to **bend and twist 'em** like we do here, but try thinking about 'em this way for a minute or two...

Now think about **drawing the card**, bent and maybe twisted, from all sorts of different angles...

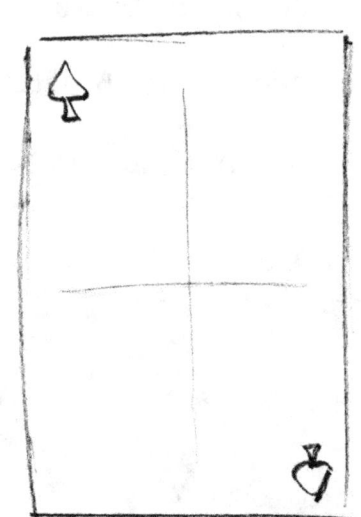
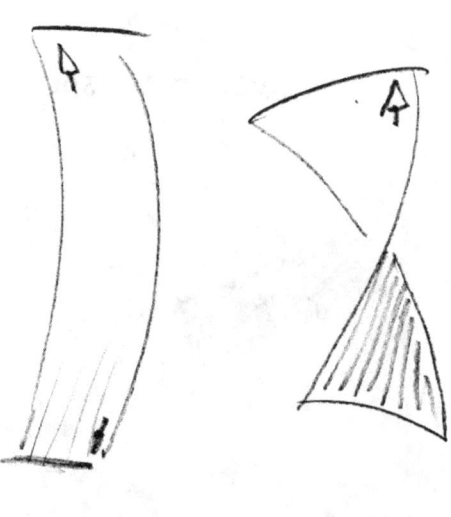
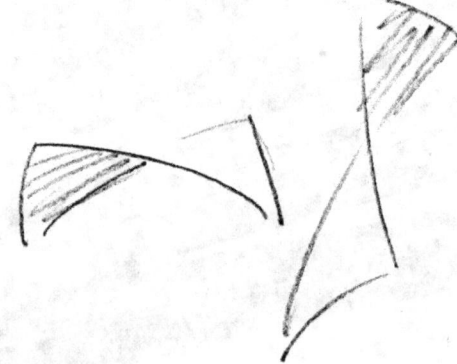
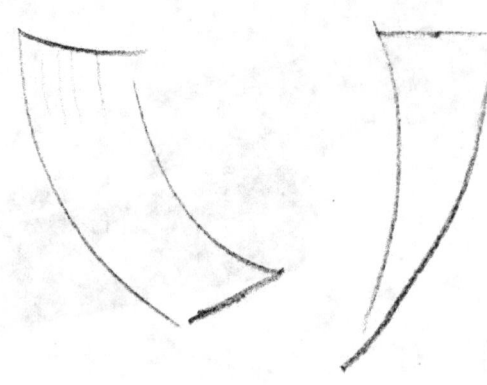
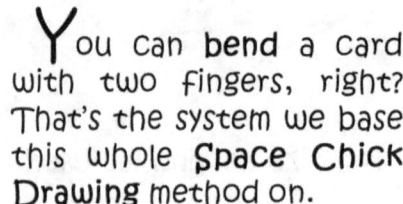
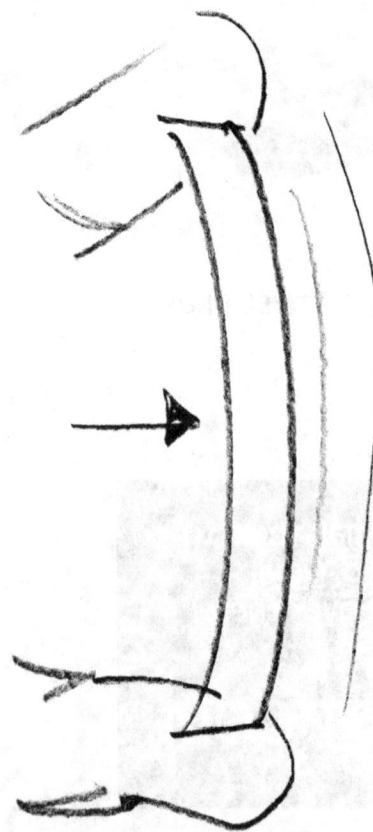

You can **bend** a card with two fingers, right? That's the system we base this whole **Space Chick Drawing** method on.

Now, imagine **two lumps** coming off the card shape, one at the **top** and one at the "ahem" BOTTOM.

Draw 'em in like so, and use a **couple more lines** to **join 'em together.**

That's going to be the **waist.**

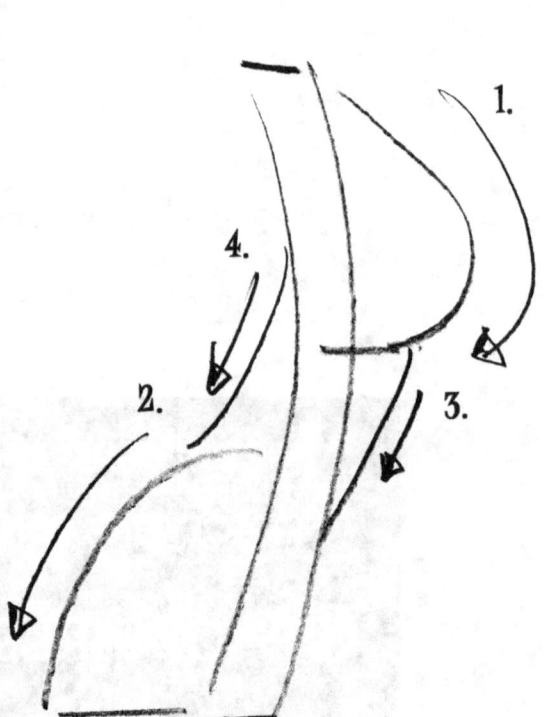

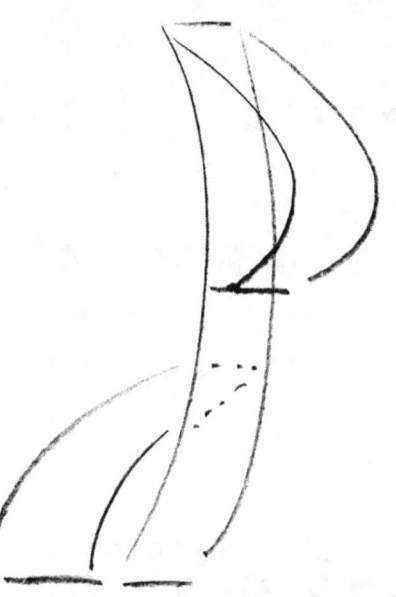

In fact, if you continue and draw in those lumps in 3-D, shown at left, you get even closer to the key to drawing sexy Space Chicks!

As you've probably guessed, these **two shapes** will form the **breasts** and the **butt**.

The **card shape** just gives you something to hang them on!

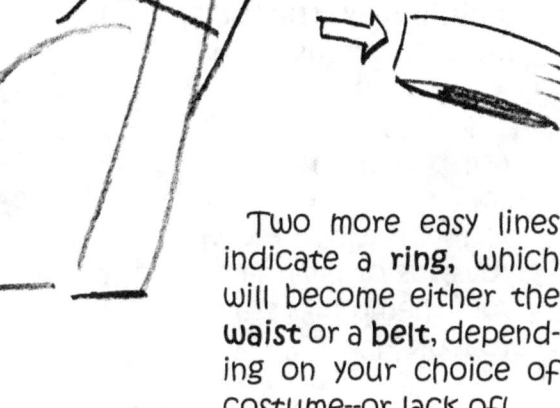

1.

2.

Two more easy lines indicate a **ring**, which will become either the **waist** or a **belt**, depending on your choice of costume--or lack of!

A few more quick lines flesh out the torso...

A little **bump** on the **back** gives something to attach **arms** to later

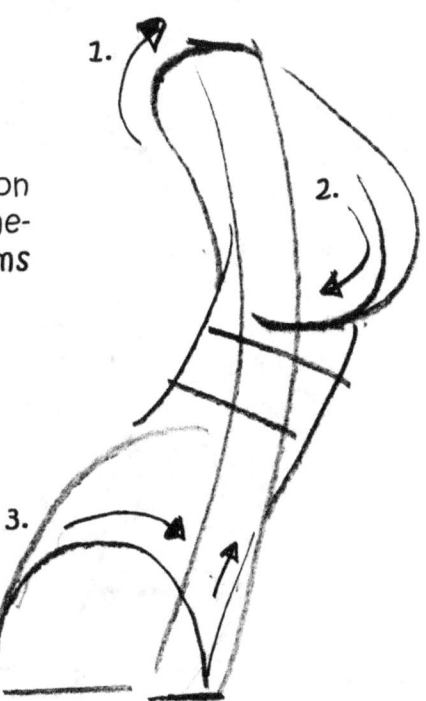

1.

2.

3.

The hip line's curved with a letter "V" at the bottom,

This is where the lady's **legs** will go!

The last line indicates the **breast** nearest the viewer--or artist!

Now you have something that resembles a dressmaker's dummy, but **rounder**!

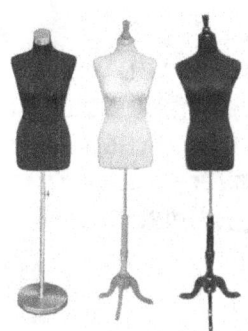

The Lollipop...

Why a **Lollipop**, you may ask?

Because depending on where the **stick** goes in, **THAT** shows which way the ball part is turning!

If you can't tell which way something's going in your drawing, either towards or away from you, then things starts to look **FLAT**.

And **Space Chicks** should never be that!

Except some of the time!

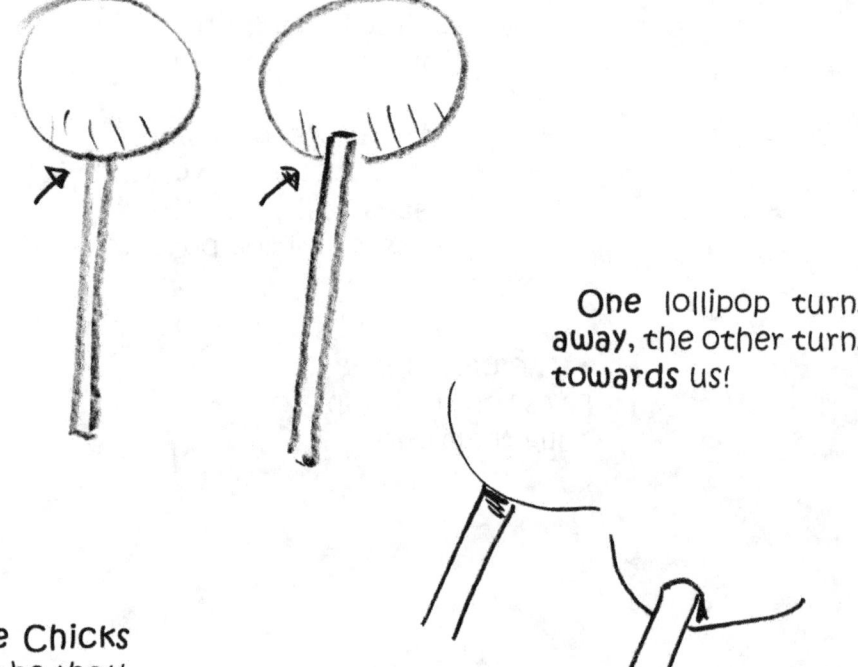

One lollipop turns **away**, the other turns **towards** us!

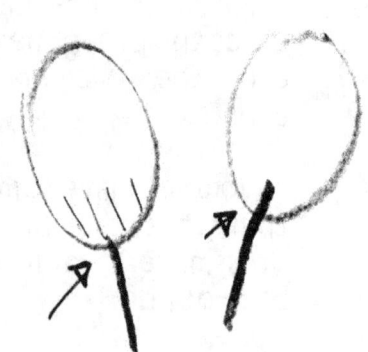

Now you've got the Lolli-pop shape down, it's real easy to make the **ball part** a little longer--into a sorta *Drumstick*.

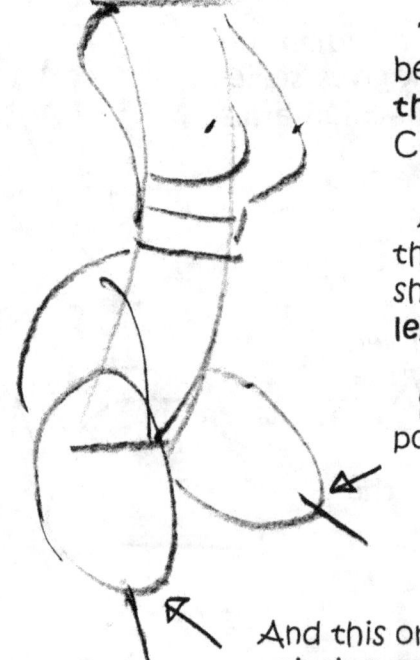

Those **Drumsticks** become the lovely **thighs** of yer Space Chick!

And notice how the **Lollipop sticks** show which way the **leg** is pointing!

See? this one's pointing **towards** us!

And this one's pointing **away**.

Now we **keep building** on what we've already got!

Four round balls show where the Space Chick's **knees** and **shoulders** are.

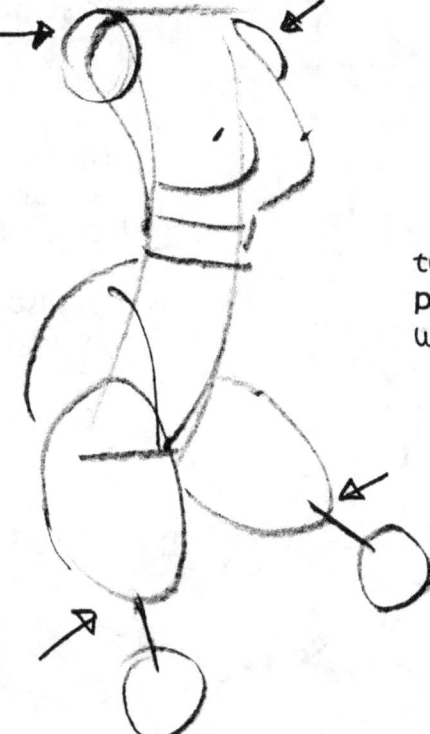

And don't worry too much about **proportions** now--just do what **feels right!**

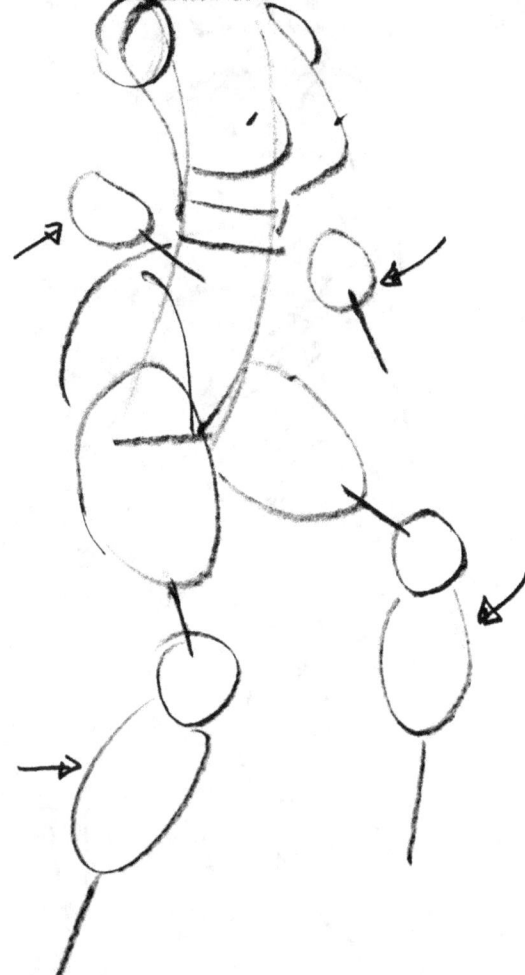

Use more **Pops** for **forearms**, just float 'em out in Space for now!

But think about what the gal might be **doing**, holding a laser pistol, or maybe leaning on a rock?

Larger Pops or **Drumsticks** become the **calves** or **lower legs**...

Again, what's she supposed to be **doing**?

You can copy **this** pose or make up your **own**, it's all up to you!

Last we add **FEET** and **HANDS**, see how **simple** these shapes are?

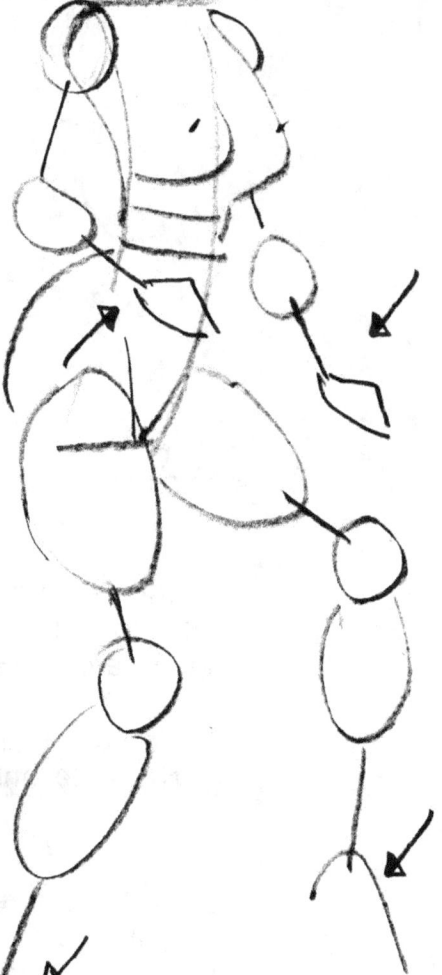

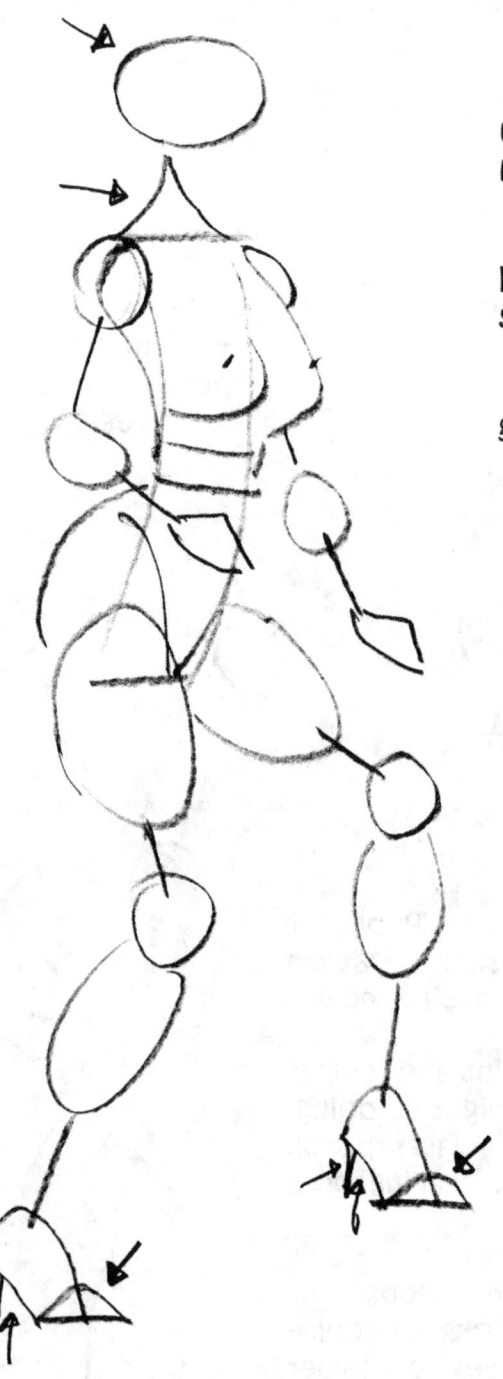

That **pointy mountain thing** coming up from the **back** is how the **spine and muscles** connect to the **skull**!

The **round part** up top represents the **brain**. You want yer Space Chick to be **smart**, right?

We also add space for where the **toes** goes, and the **high heels**.

Pretty **easy**, huh?

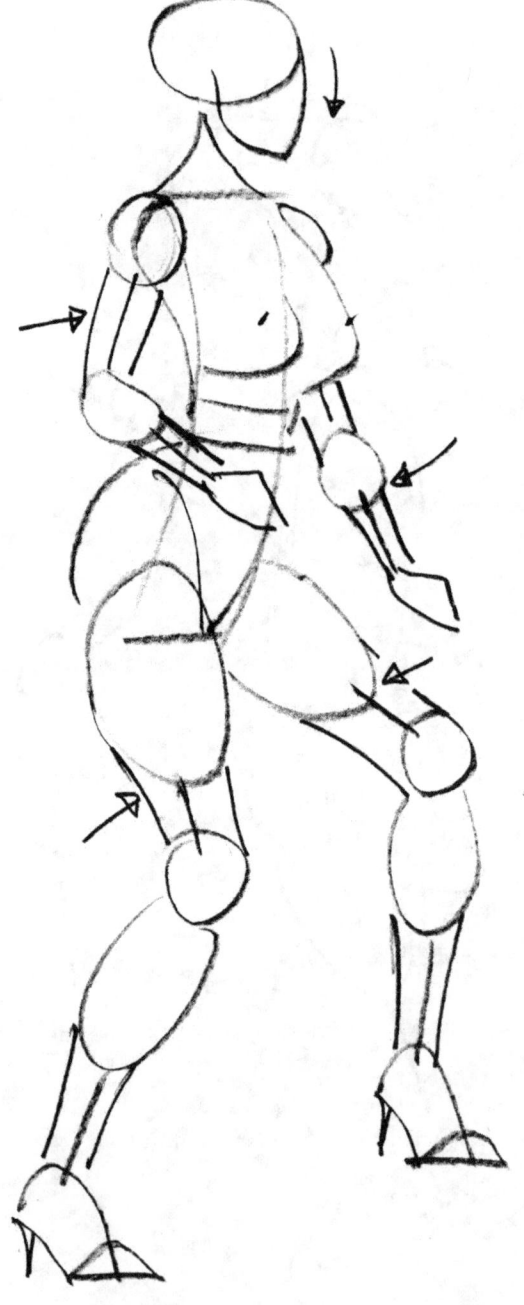

Close off the **upper arms, forearms, legs** and **calves** with more lines, sorta making 'em into **tubes**.

A line down the front of the brain is for the **face**, and another is for the **jaw**.

If you just **gotta** jump ahead to the **face**, here's how to draw it:

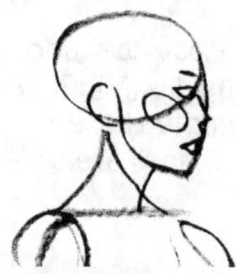

Head & Shoulders Above

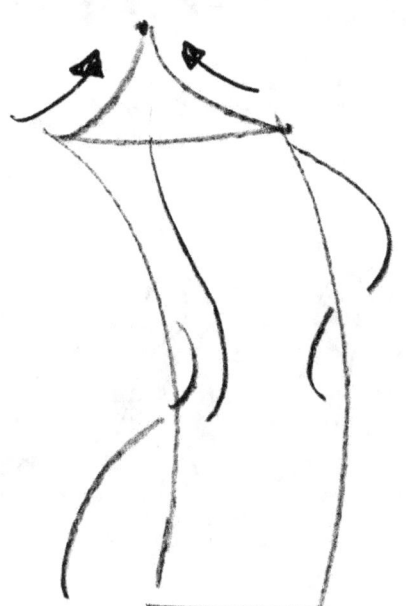

You can see how **easy** the Space Chick **body** is to draw now!

But, she will need a **head**, so at your left is a simple method for drawing how the **Tra-pezius muscles** go from the **back** to the base of the **skull**.

Also note at right: how the **neck** view **changes** seen from the **front**.

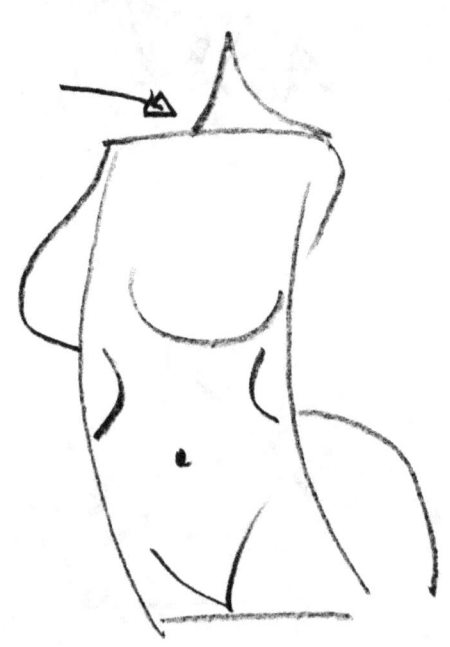

At left is a bigger view of the **neck** and upper body, all still based on that simple **Playing Card** foundation!

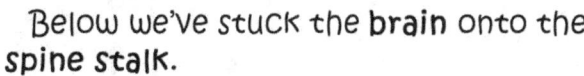

Below we've stuck the **brain** onto the **spine stalk**.

The brain will actually become the **brain-case** of the **skull**...

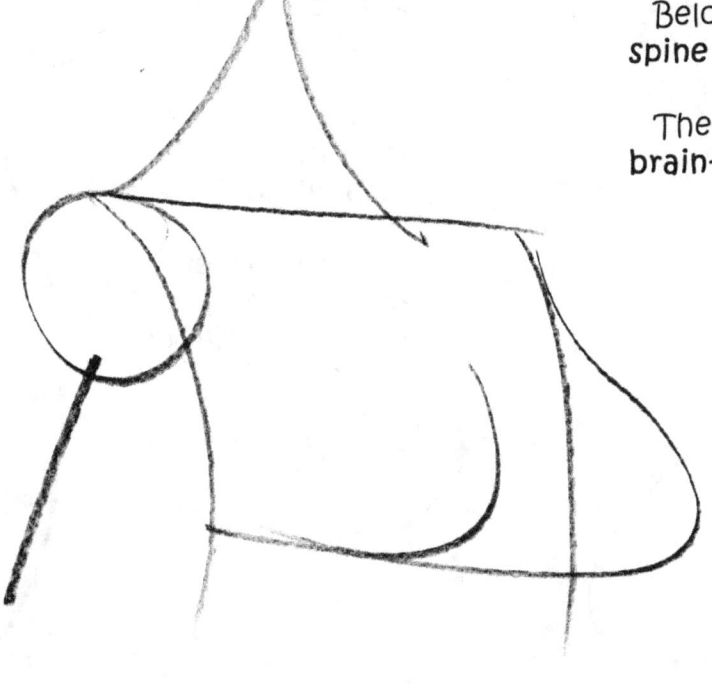

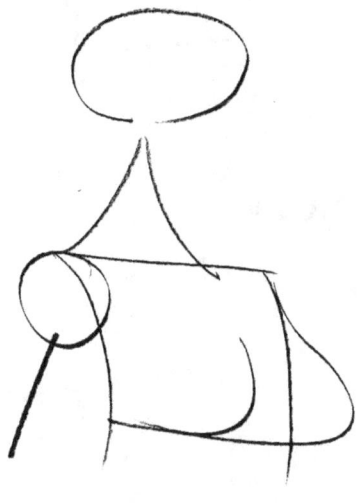

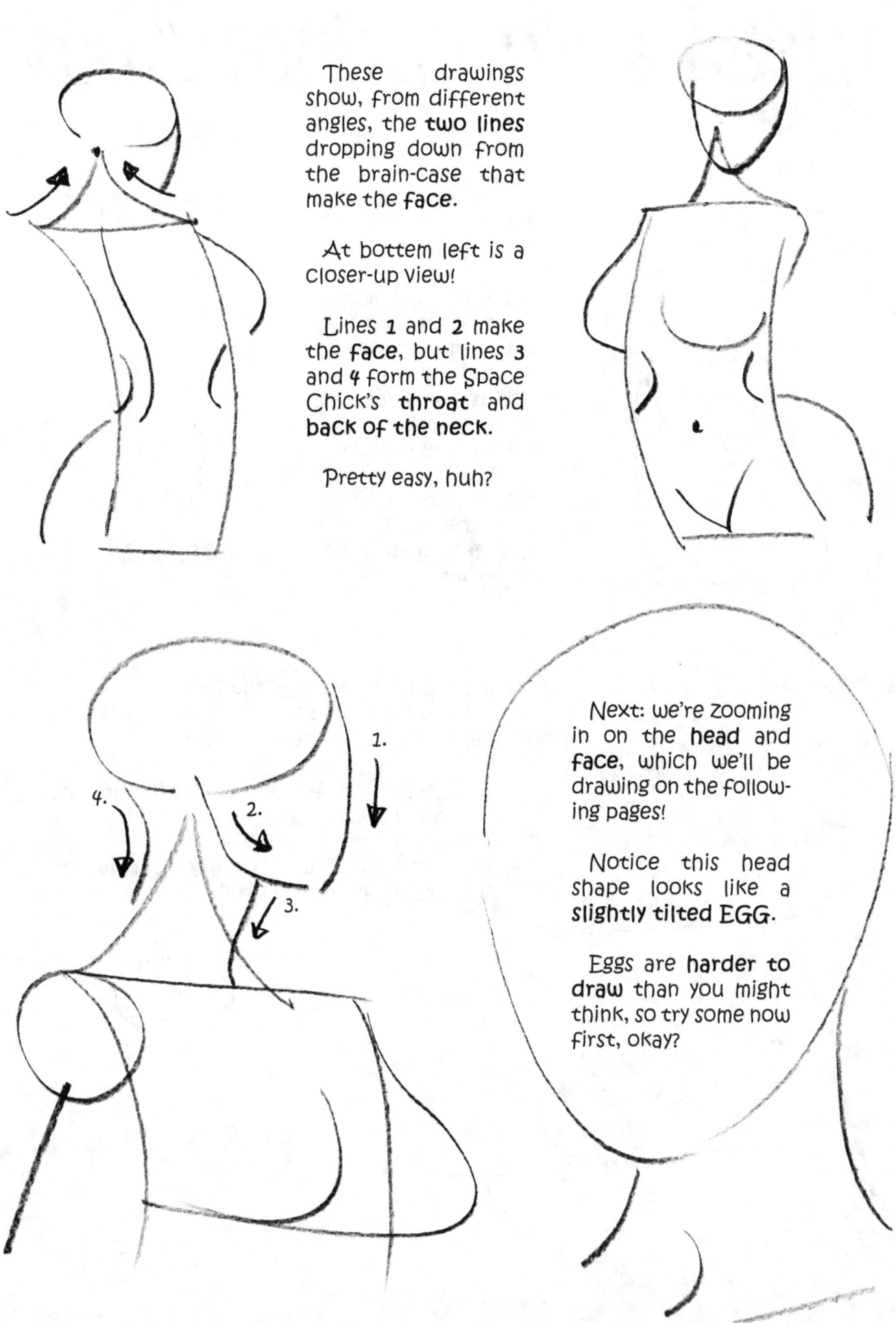

These drawings show, from different angles, the **two lines** dropping down from the brain-case that make the **face**.

At bottom left is a closer-up view!

Lines **1** and **2** make the **face**, but lines **3** and **4** form the Space Chick's **throat** and **back of the neck**.

Pretty easy, huh?

1.

2.

3.

4.

Next: we're zooming in on the **head** and **face**, which we'll be drawing on the following pages!

Notice this head shape looks like a **slightly tilted EGG**.

Eggs are **harder to draw** than you might think, so try some now first, okay?

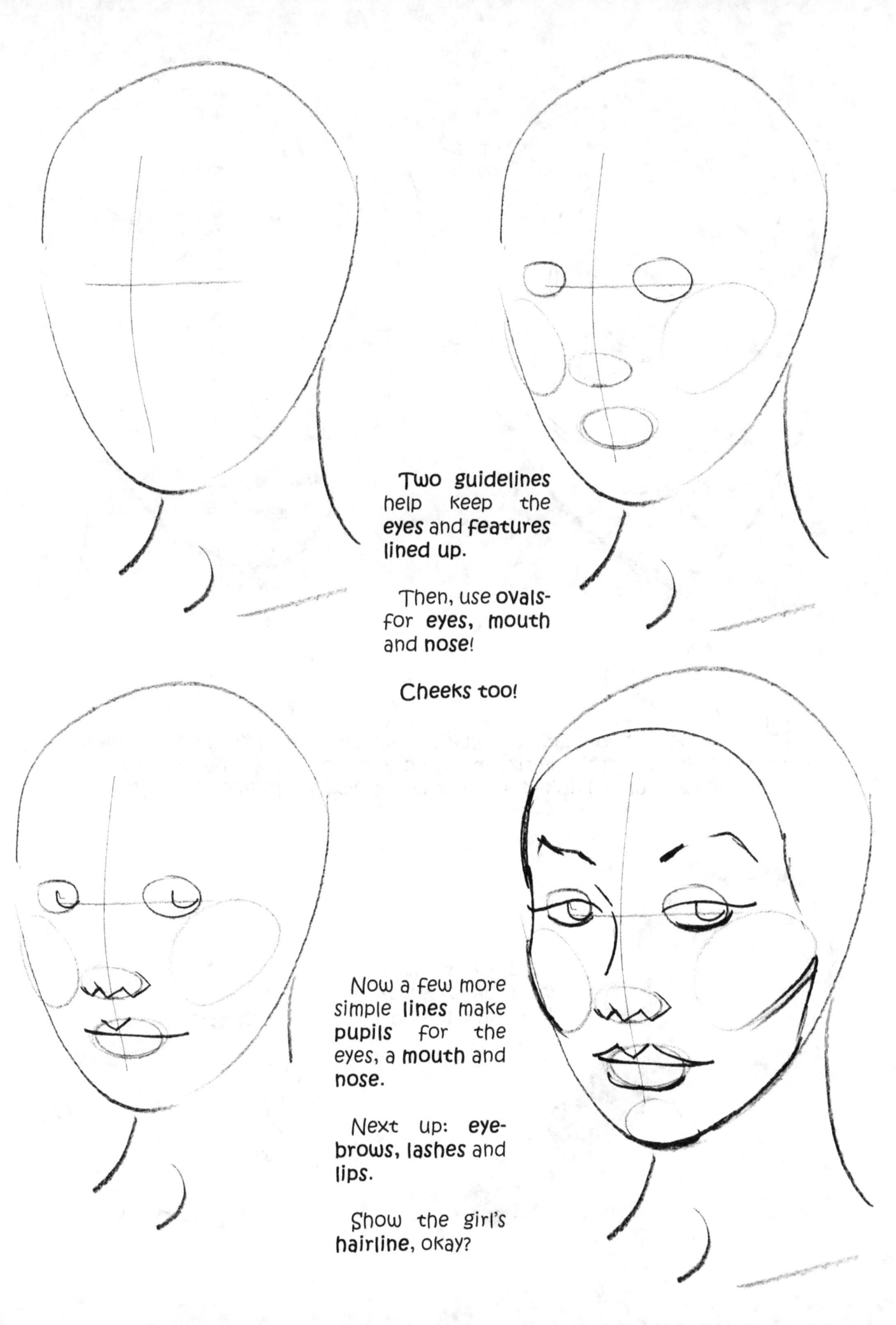

Two guidelines help keep the **eyes** and **features** lined up.

Then, use **ovals**-for **eyes**, **mouth** and **nose**!

Cheeks too!

Now a few more simple **lines** make **pupils** for the eyes, a **mouth** and **nose**.

Next up: **eye-brows**, **lashes** and **lips**.

Show the girl's **hairline**, okay?

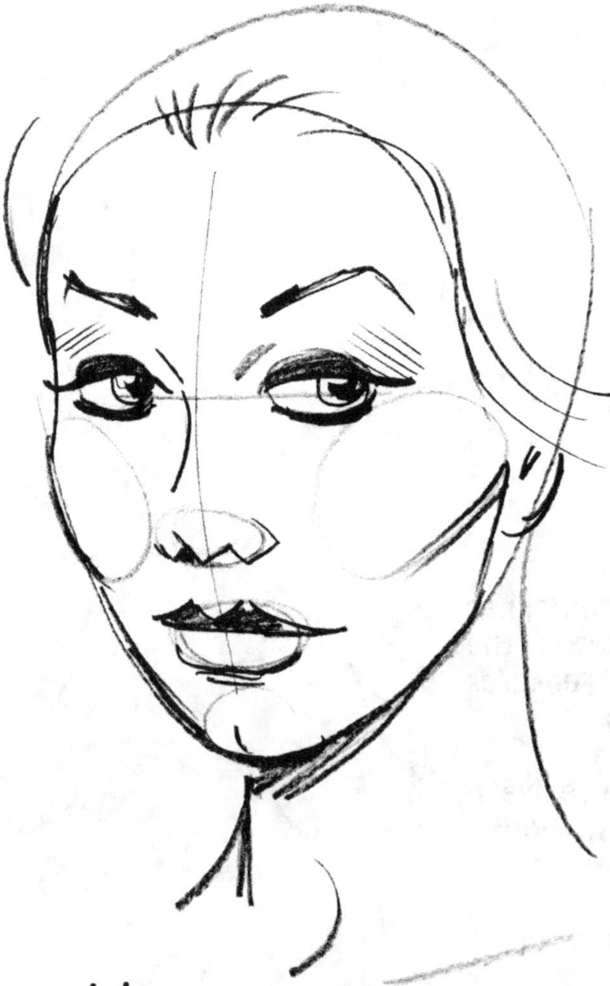

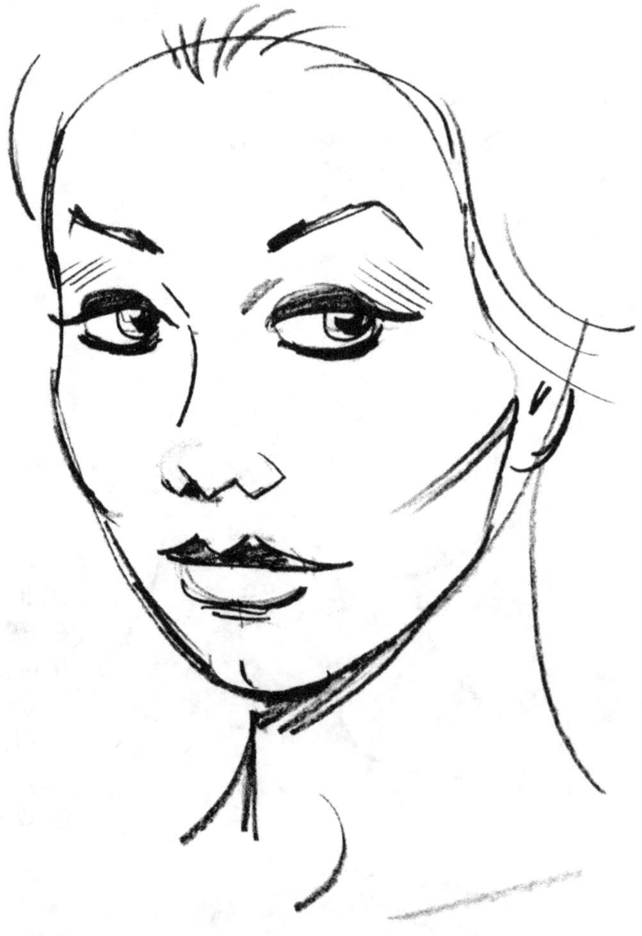

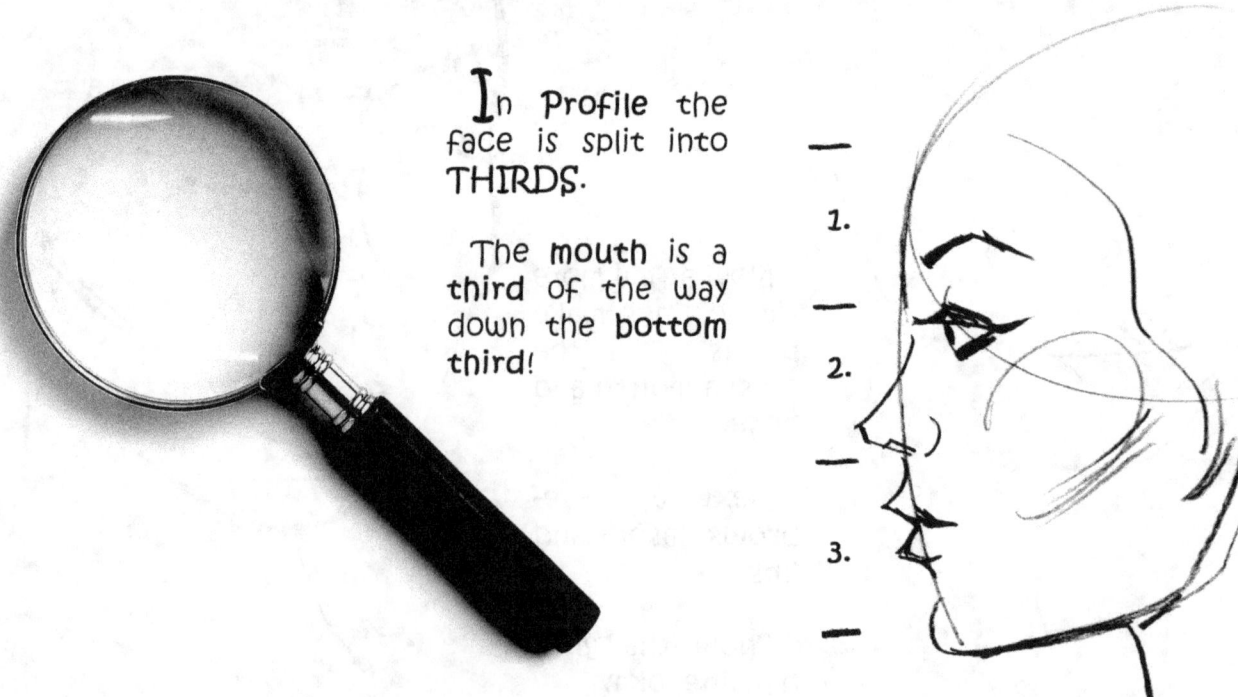

Here's the **finished head**, with guidelines erased, ready for **inking**! You may not do all your heads this **big size**, but if they're pretty **small** then you might use Mike's Secret Trick--draw them with a MAGNIFYING GLASS!

In **Profile** the face is split into THIRDS.

The **mouth** is a **third** of the way down the **bottom third**!

—
1.
—
2.
—
3.
—

Pokey-ness

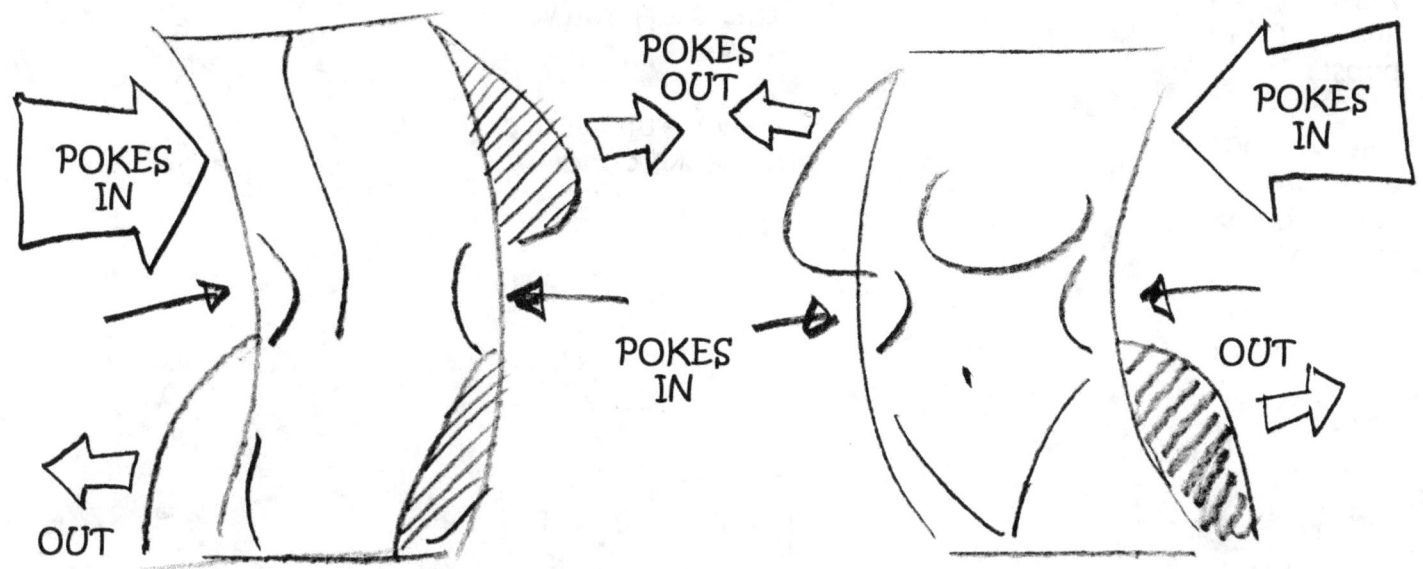

The true **Secret of Drawing**, and the entire Universe for that matter, is that *stuff either pokes IN or it pokes OUT.* You can clearly see that here for yourself!

These drawings show our **Dressmaker Dummy** or **Torso**, still built on the simple **Playing Card** form! The better you get at this simple shape **now**, the **faster** and **better** you'll be able to draw your **own Space Chicks** later!

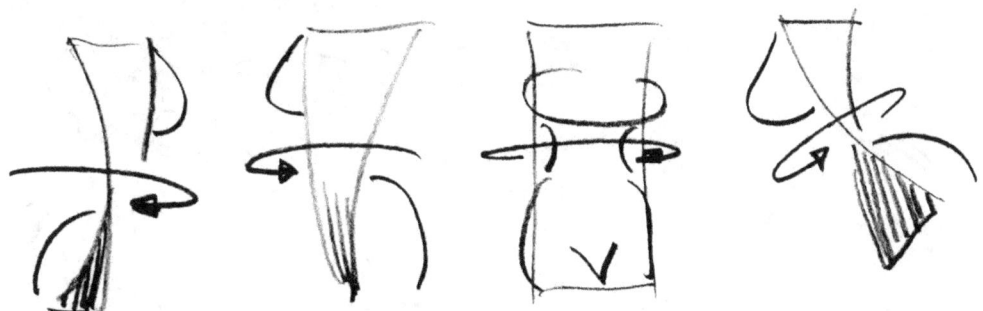

Now you're probably ready to start trying **lots more** interesting **angles** for your **Space Chick bodies!**

Always **start** building with the **Playing Card first**, then **twist** and **turn** that thing, maybe with the final pose in mind or maybe not!

Remember: **Drawing** always **starts simple** and then gets more **complicated** as you **add stuff.**

But the **real** beauty of these beauties is: **A GOOD TORSO IS ALMOST IMPOSSIBLE TO RUIN BY ADDING ARMS AND LEGS!**

Demonstration #1

Start with **Playing Card** and **Lolli-pops**!

Add lines and circles for back-ground.

Draw in all the other stuff you've learned!

Have fun with the background!

Use a **brush marker** for **blacks**, put them everywhere you want people to **look**.

Then use a **fine marker** for. every-thing else!

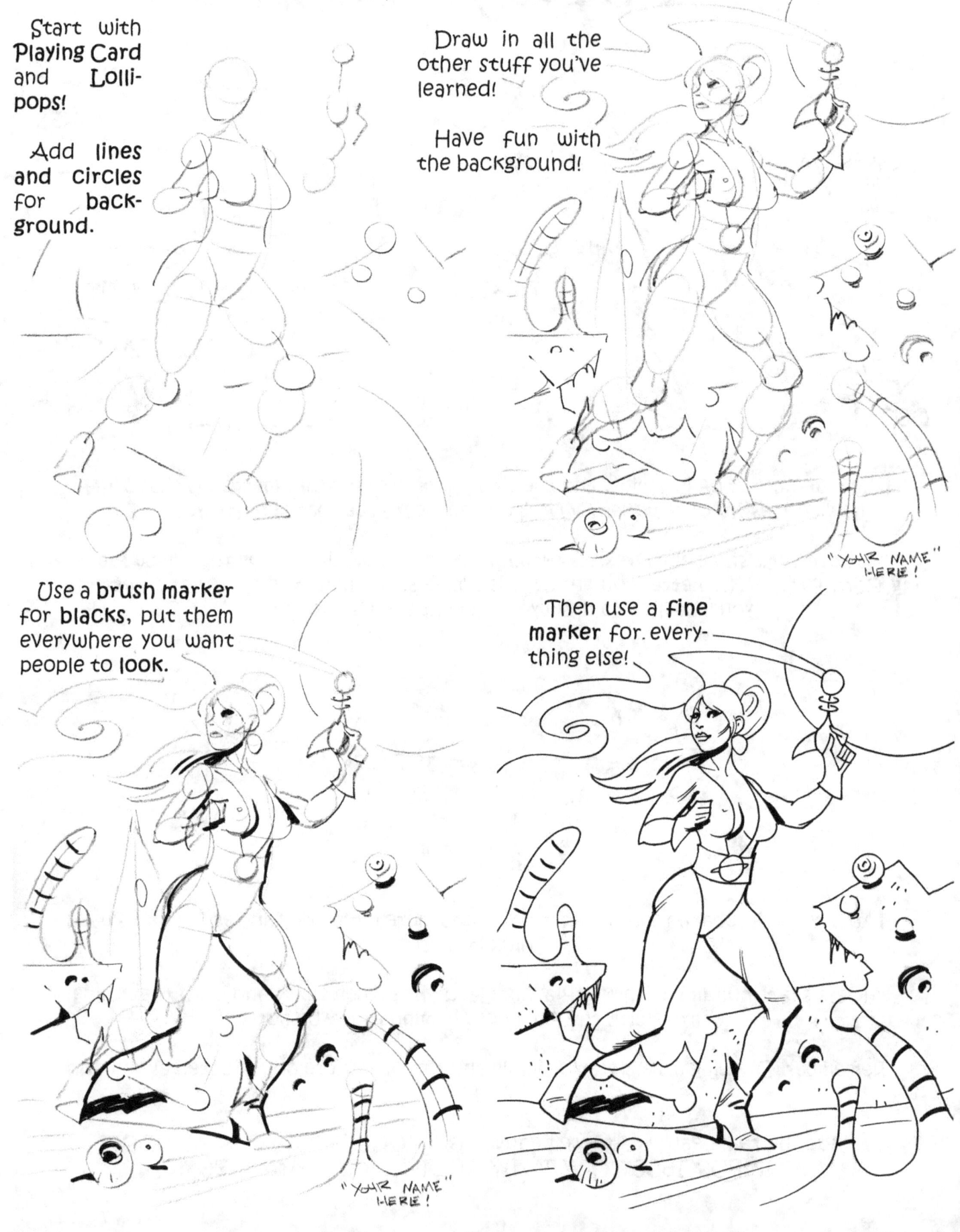

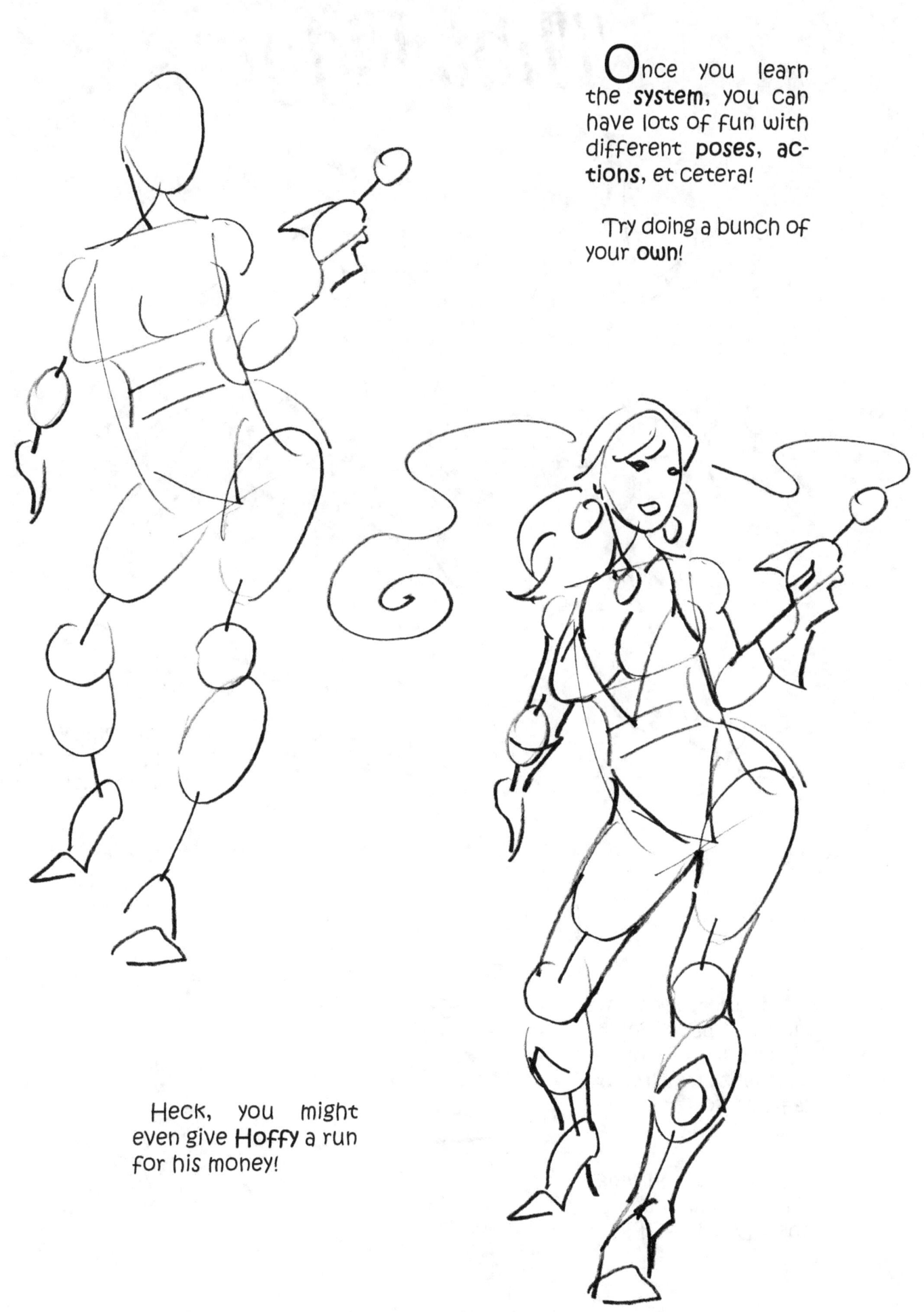

Once you learn the **system**, you can have lots of fun with different **poses**, ac-tions, et cetera!

Try doing a bunch of your **own**!

Heck, you might even give **Hoffy** a run for his money!

That Figgers...

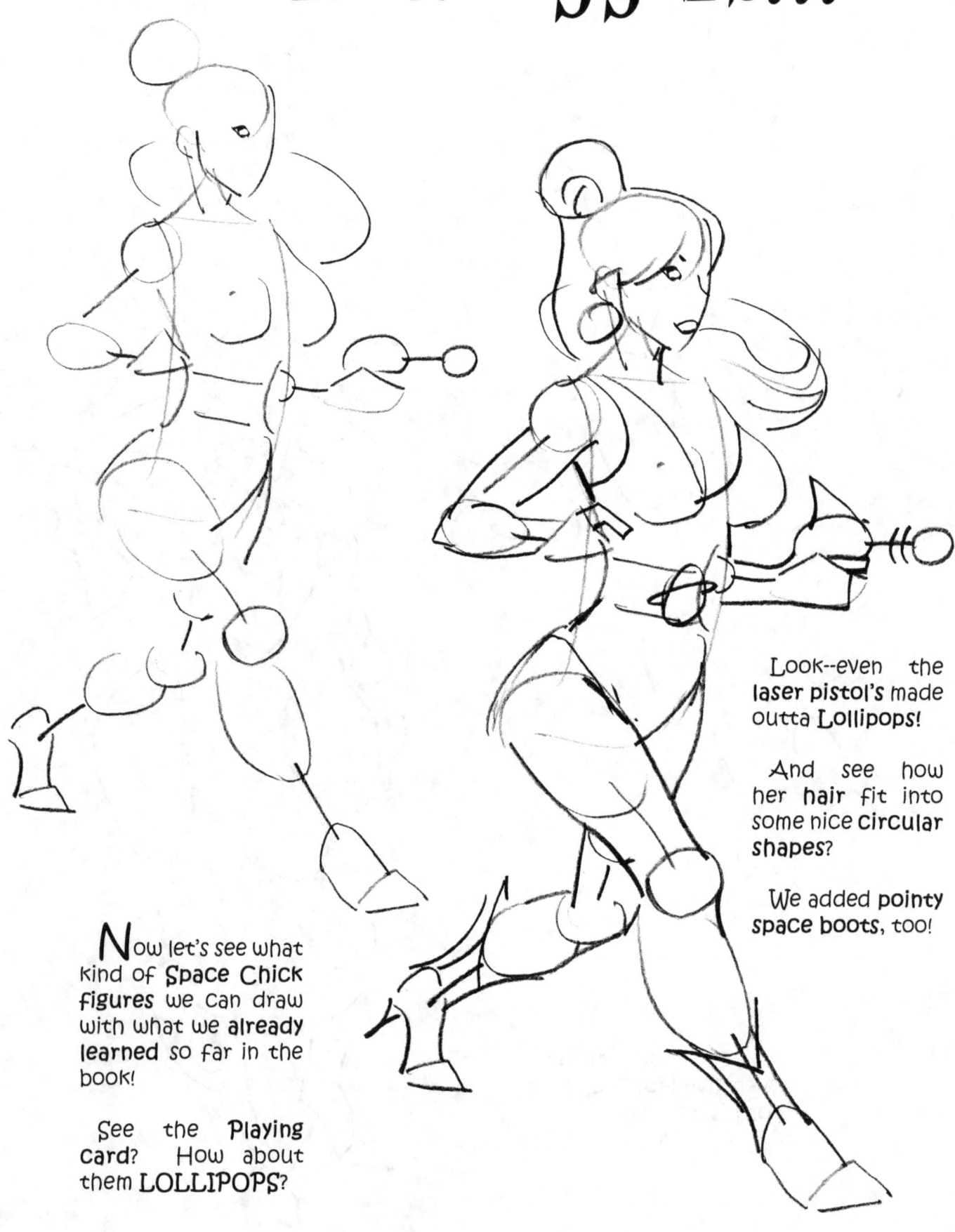

Look--even the laser pistol's made outta **Lollipops!**

And see how her **hair** fit into some nice **circular shapes?**

We added **pointy space boots**, too!

Now let's see what kind of **Space Chick figures** we can draw with what we **already learned** so far in the book!

See the **Playing card?** How about them **LOLLIPOPS?**

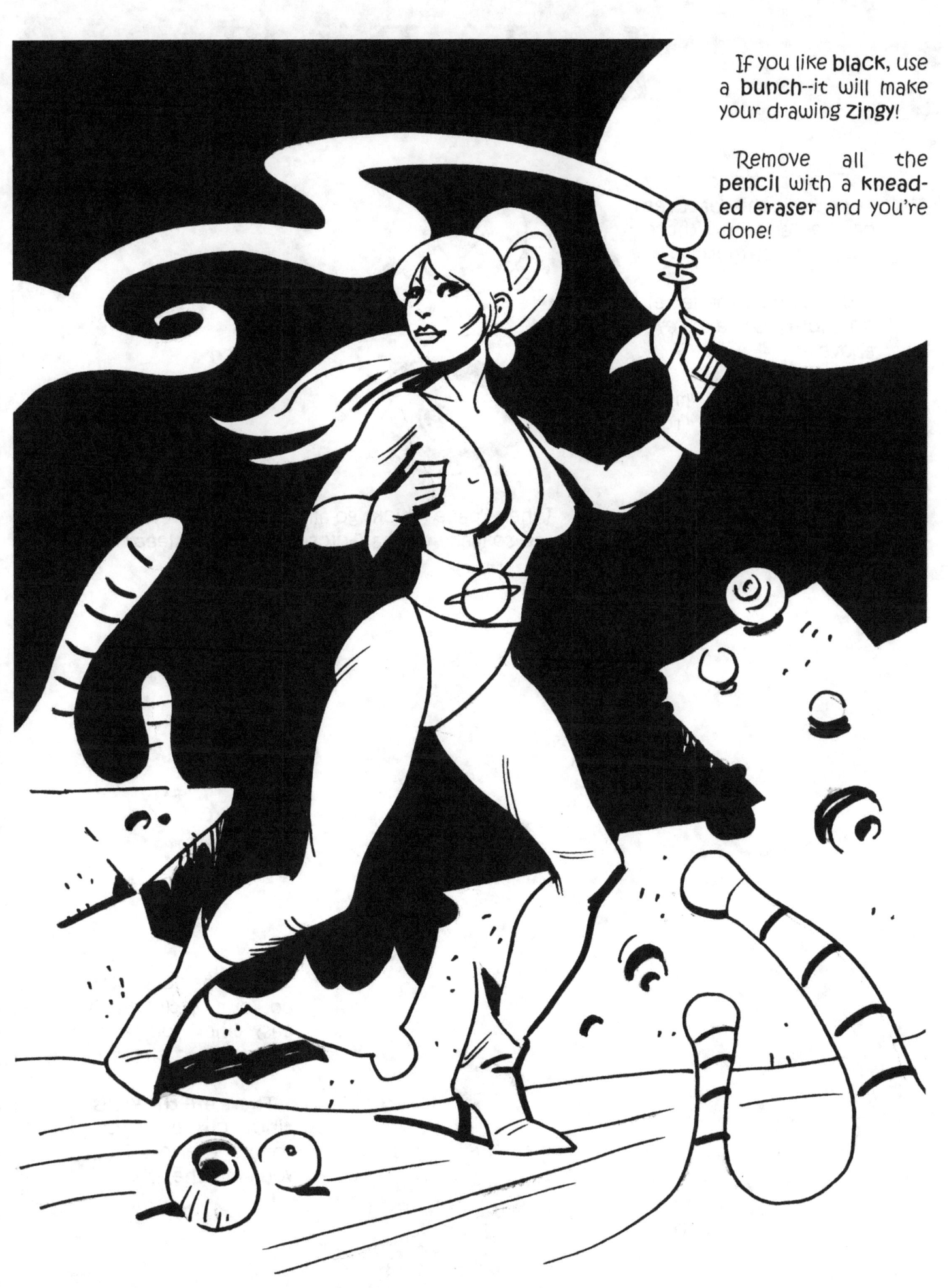

If you like **black**, use a **bunch**--it will make your drawing **zingy**!

Remove all the **pencil** with a **kneaded eraser** and you're done!

In the Details

Here's some easy ways to fit the **features** of the **face** into those **ovals and circles**!

Notice how the letter "O" **mouth** is like the **eye** above it?

In **Space**, most everything's made from **circles**!

The cute **nose** below is like two letter "W"s stuck together.

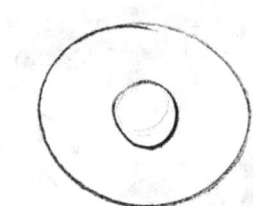 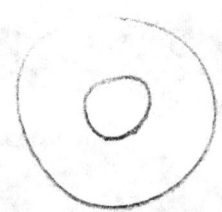

When Space Chicks go all **gooshy**, their **eyes show it**, so make the **half-closed lid** sorta "sleepy"...

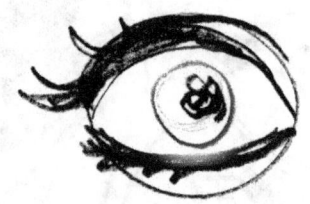 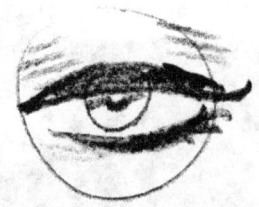

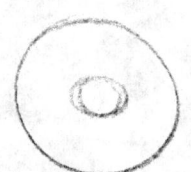

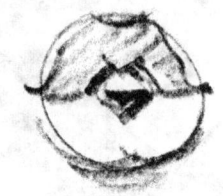

Even the complicated form of the **ear** is easy when you break it down into **circles**!

There are **three distinct circles** in the ear to the left-- can you **find them**?

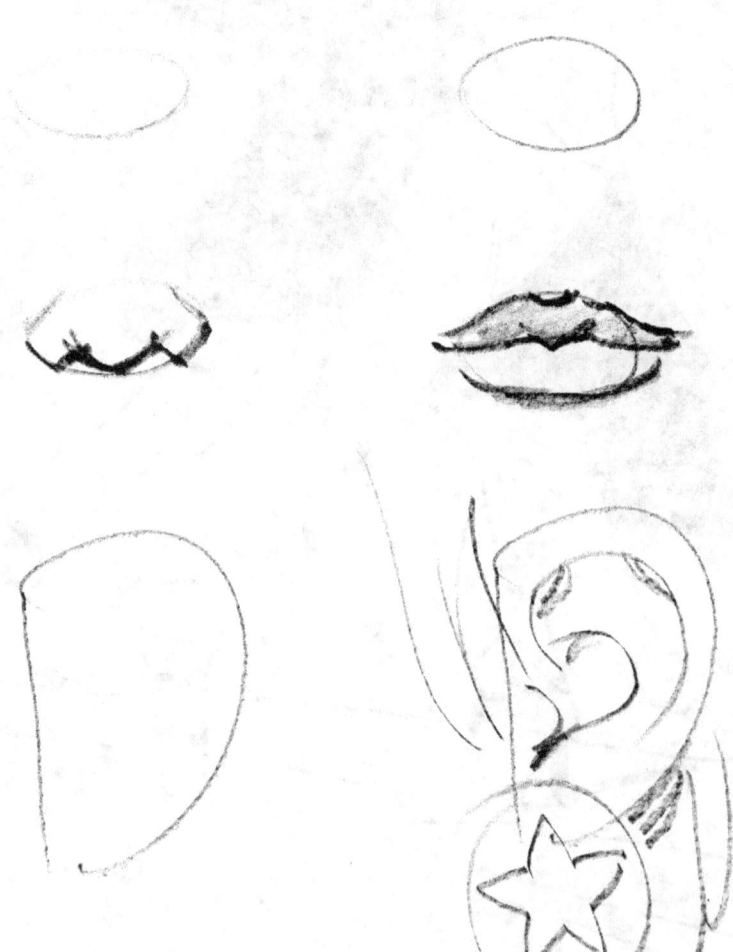

Tougher Poses

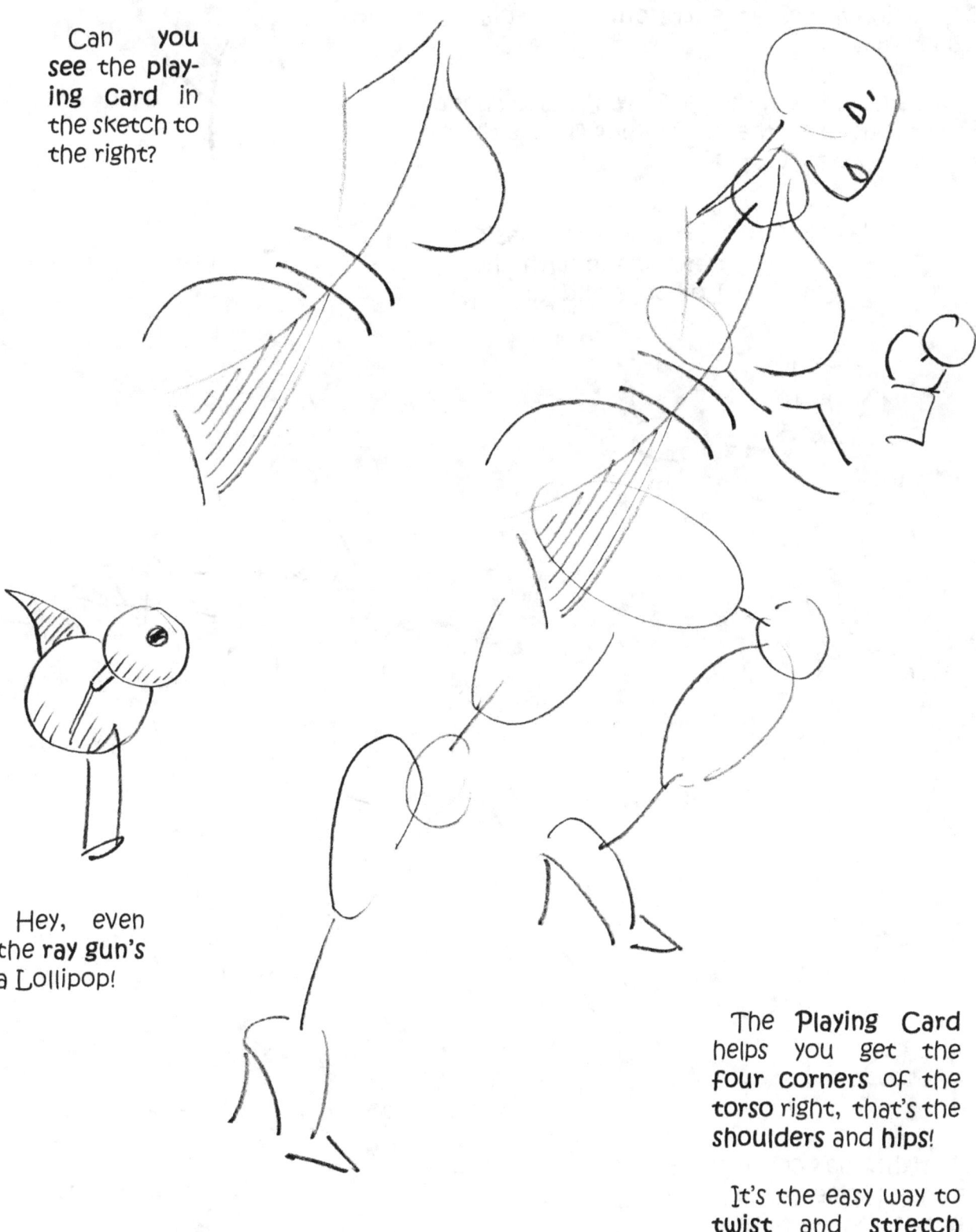

Can **you** *see* the play-ing card in the sketch to the right?

Hey, even the **ray gun's** a Lollipop!

The **Playing Card** helps you get the **four corners** of the **torso** right, that's the **shoulders** and **hips!**

It's the easy way to **twist** and **stretch** your girl in Space!

Extra Twist

You can maximize the Twisting in your Space Girls, which makes 'em extra curvy, especially in zero gravity!

Notice he we used the old Playing Card shape, at right, but drew the heavy lines first with the patented Extra Twist "X"!

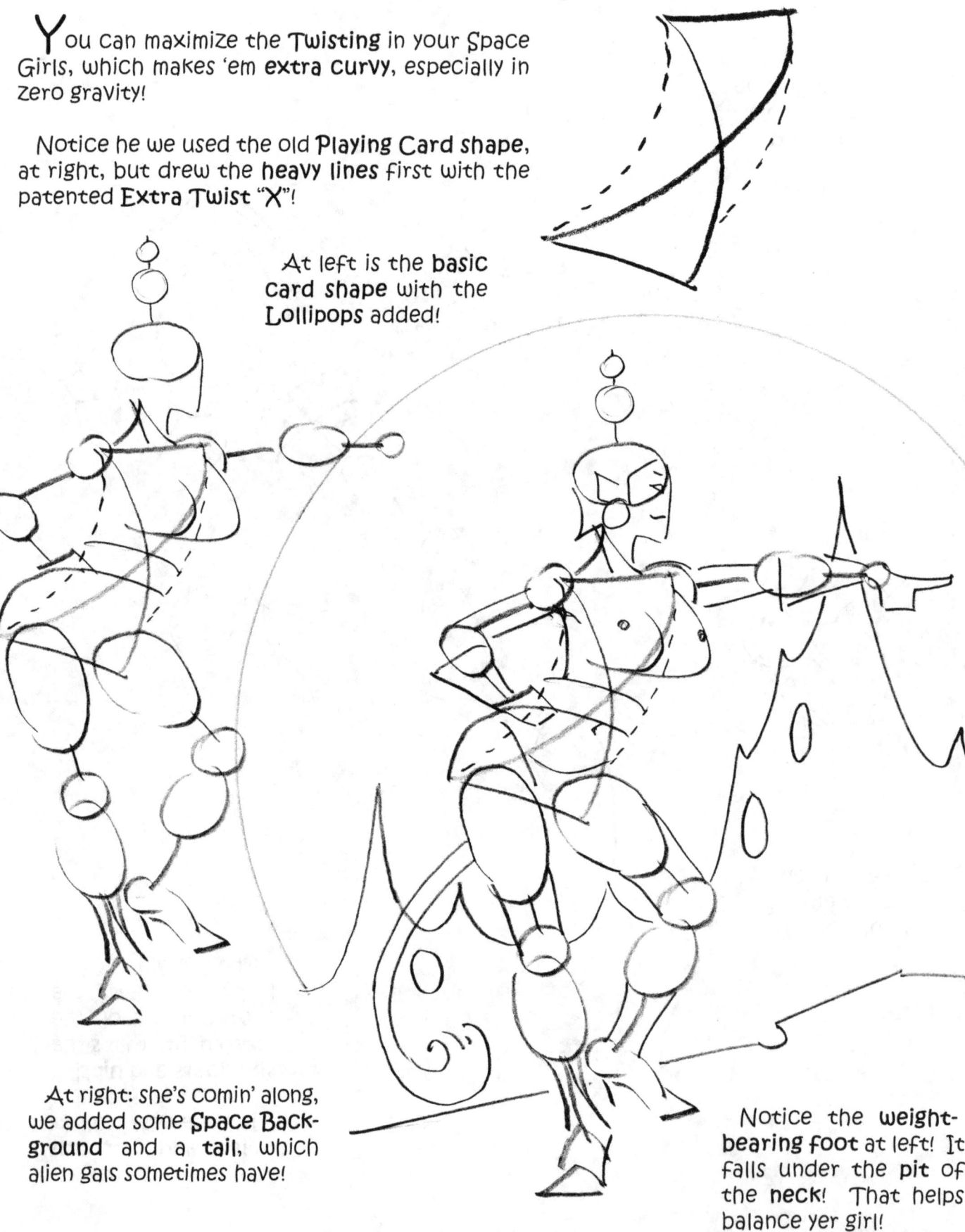

At left is the basic card shape with the Lollipops added!

At right: she's comin' along, we added some Space Background and a tail, which alien gals sometimes have!

Notice the weight-bearing foot at left! It falls under the pit of the neck! That helps balance yer girl!

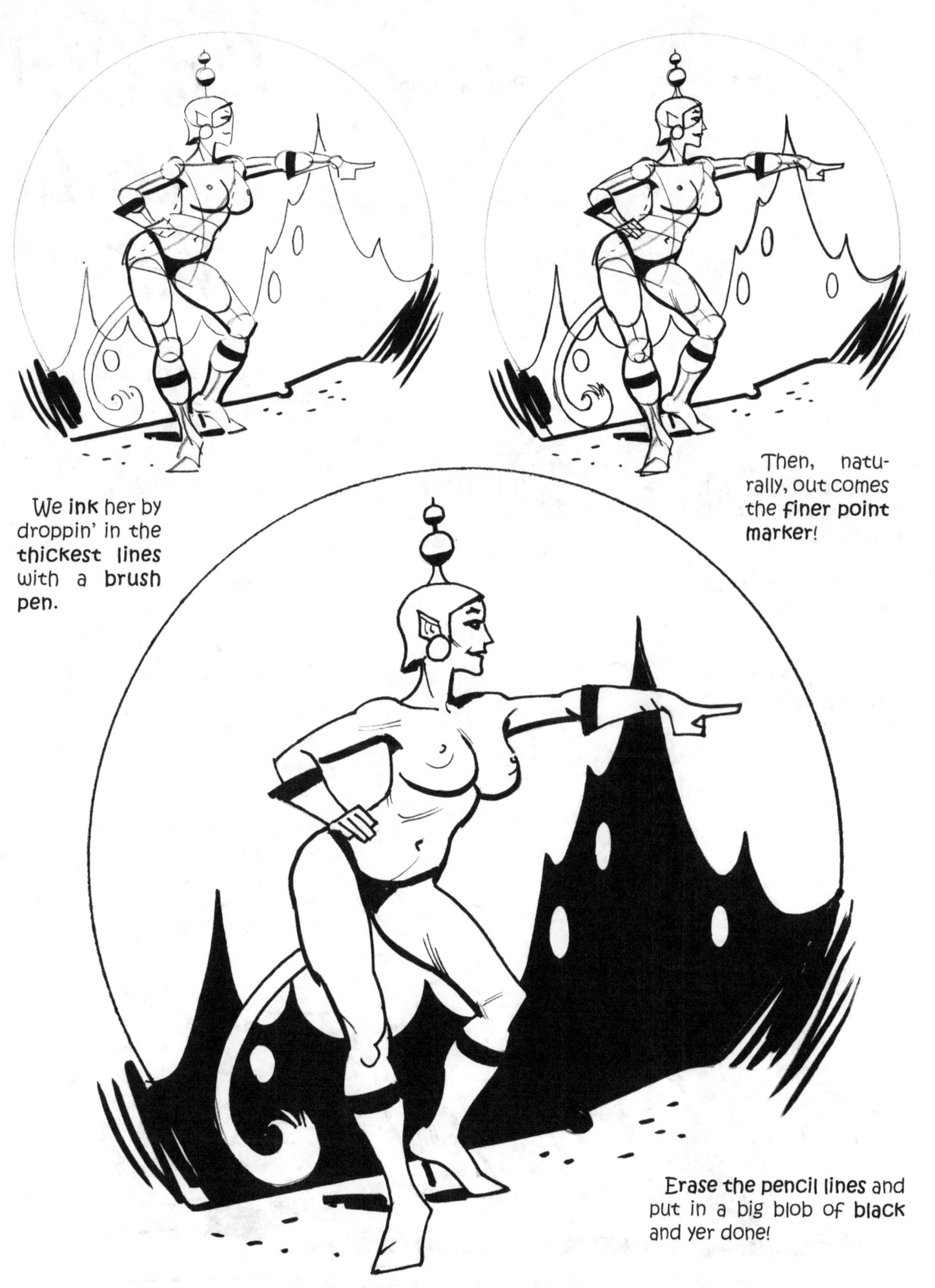

We ink her by droppin' in the **thickest lines** with a **brush pen**.

Then, naturally, out comes the **finer point marker!**

Erase the pencil lines and put in a big blob of **black** and yer done!

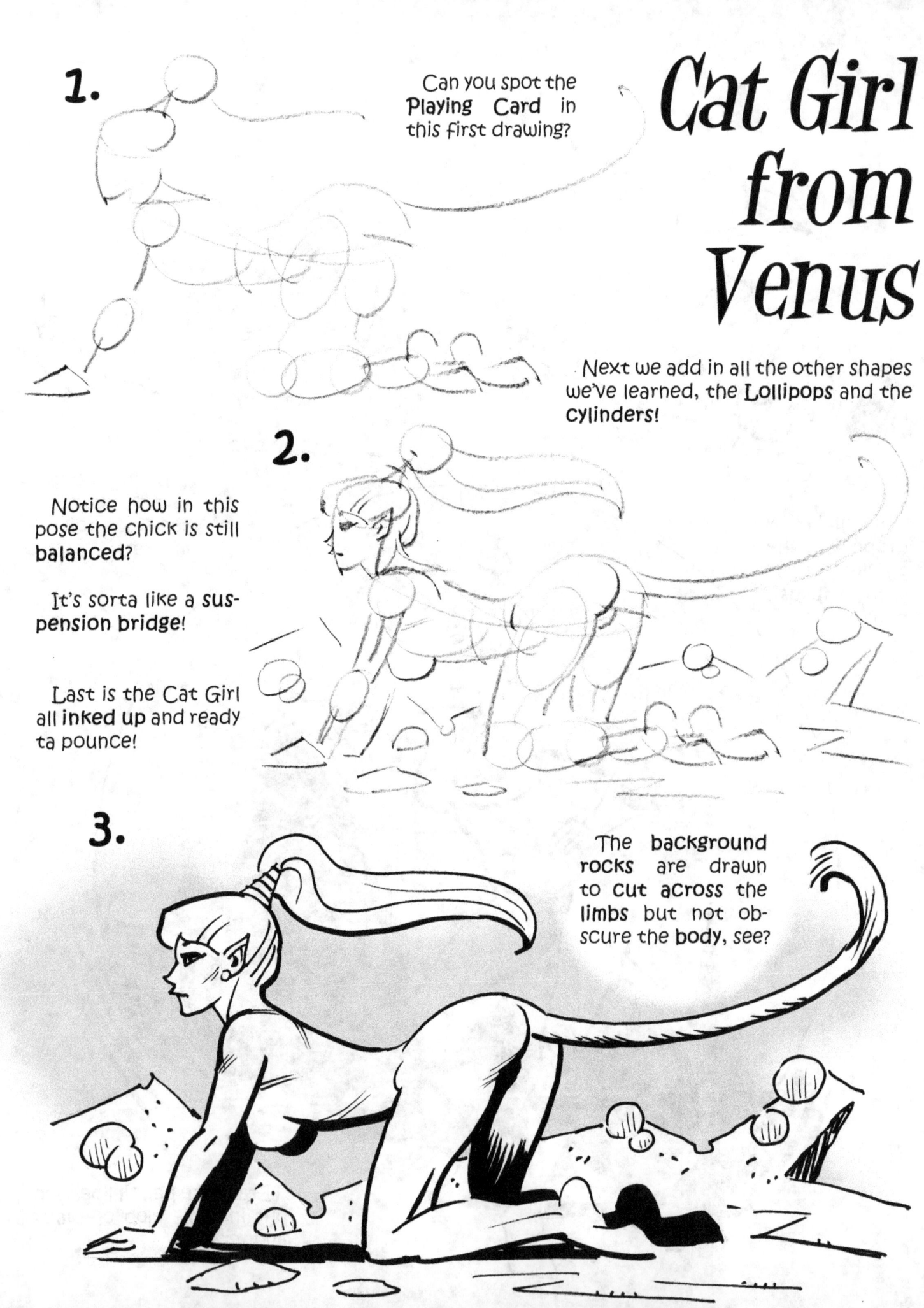

1.

Can you spot the **Playing Card** in this first drawing?

Cat Girl from Venus

Next we add in all the other shapes we've learned, the **Lollipops** and the **cylinders!**

2.

Notice how in this pose the chick is still **balanced?**

It's sorta like a **suspension bridge!**

Last is the Cat Girl all **inked up** and ready ta pounce!

3.

The **background rocks** are drawn to **cut across** the **limbs** but not obscure the **body**, see?

Getting Around

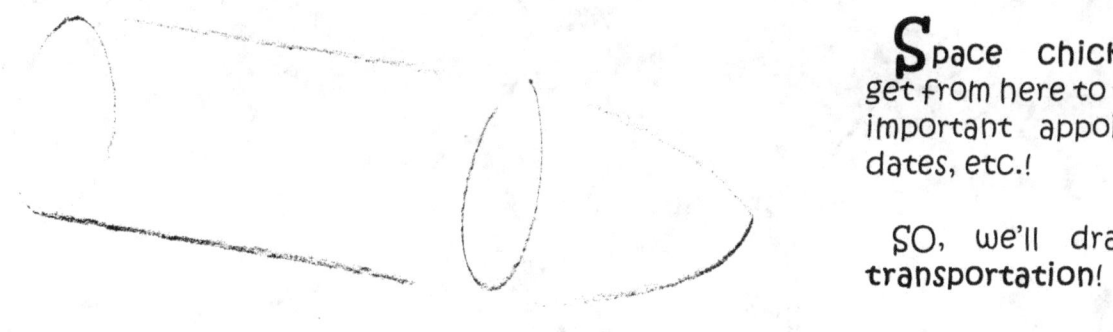

Space chicks gotta get from here to there for important appointments, dates, etc.!

SO, we'll draw some transportation!

Jusr start with a simple Tube, then put a round nose on the front.

Next ya turn it into a sorta bedroom slipper with a front and a thick sole.

The back part is just a piece of the tube.

Go ahead and stick on the windshield.

A few other simple shapes make the fins, tailpipe and a seat.

Your chick's gotta sit some- where, remember?

And we even stuck a little grill on the front!

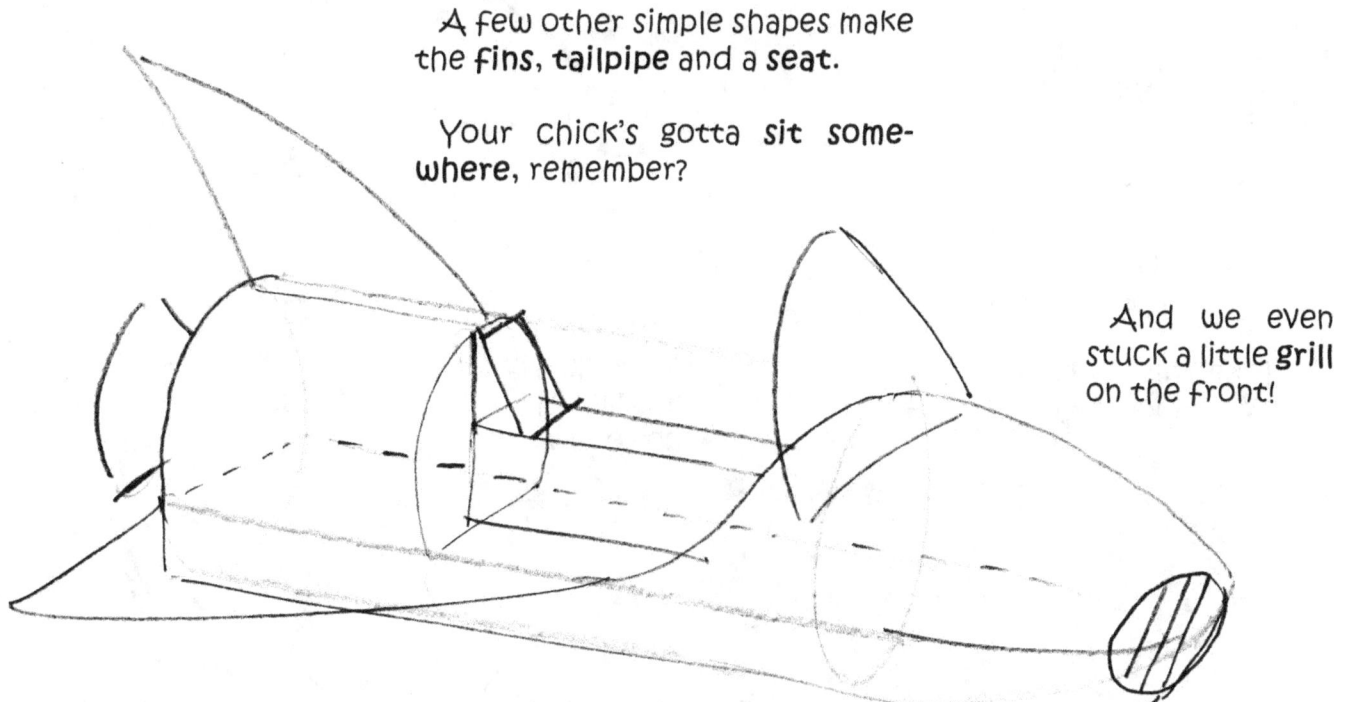

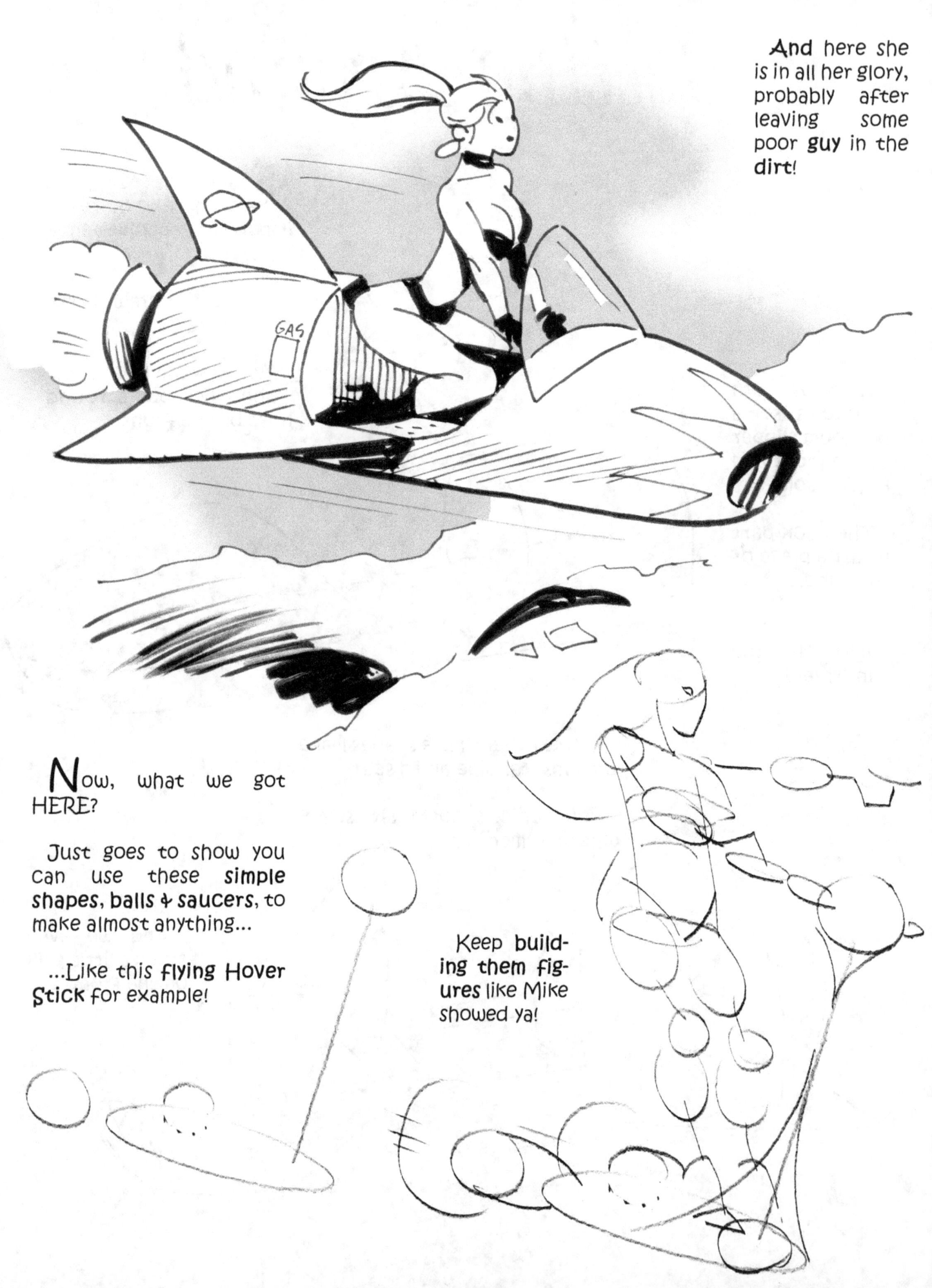

And here she is in all her glory, probably after leaving some poor **guy** in the **dirt**!

Now, what we got **HERE**?

Just goes to show you can use these **simple shapes, balls & saucers**, to make almost anything...

...Like this **flying Hover Stick** for example!

Keep build-ing them **fig-ures** like Mike showed ya!

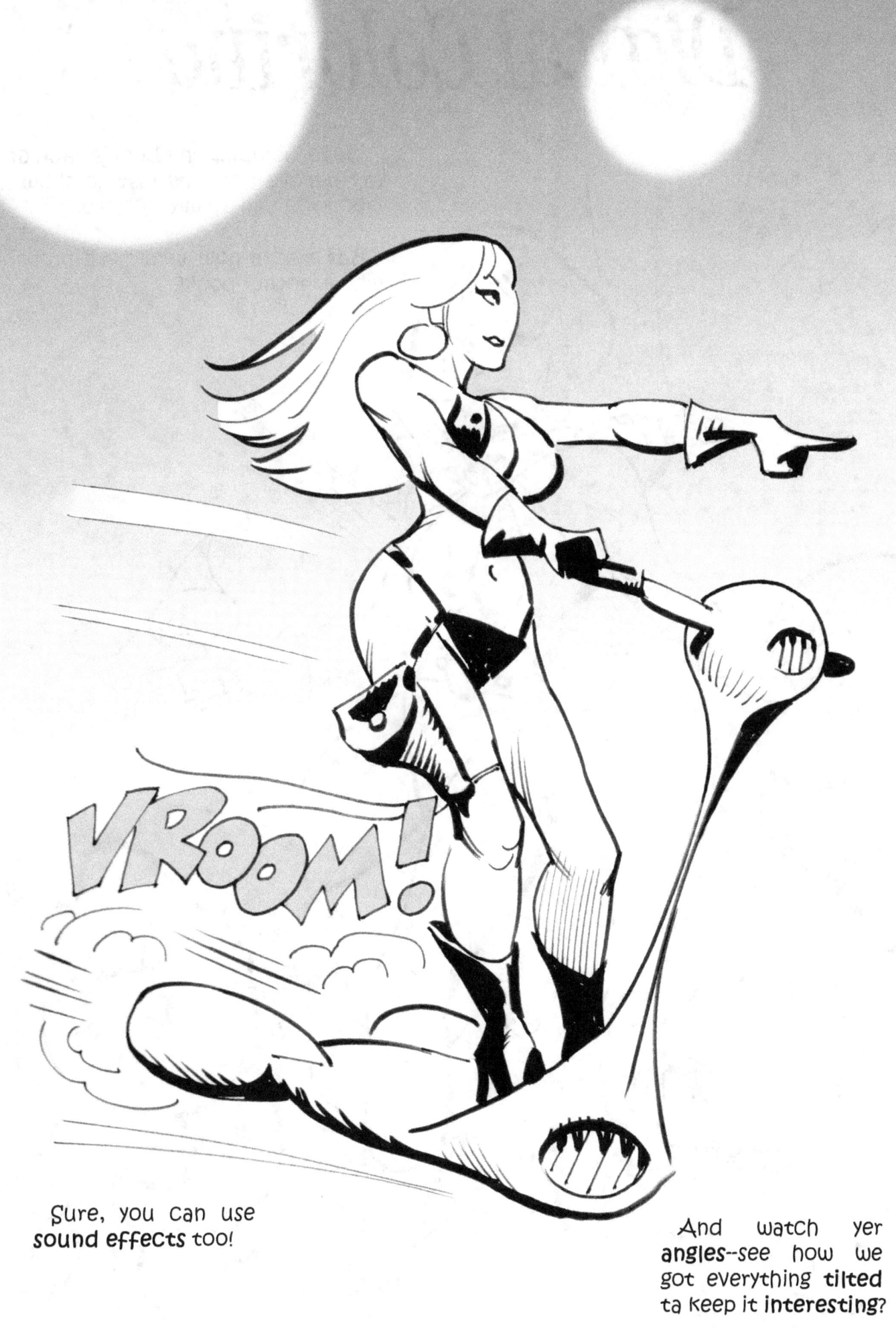

Digital Coloring

We're including this book's **back cover art before coloring** just to show how much you can do with **Photoshop!**

But exactly how we did it is probably a whole 'nother book!

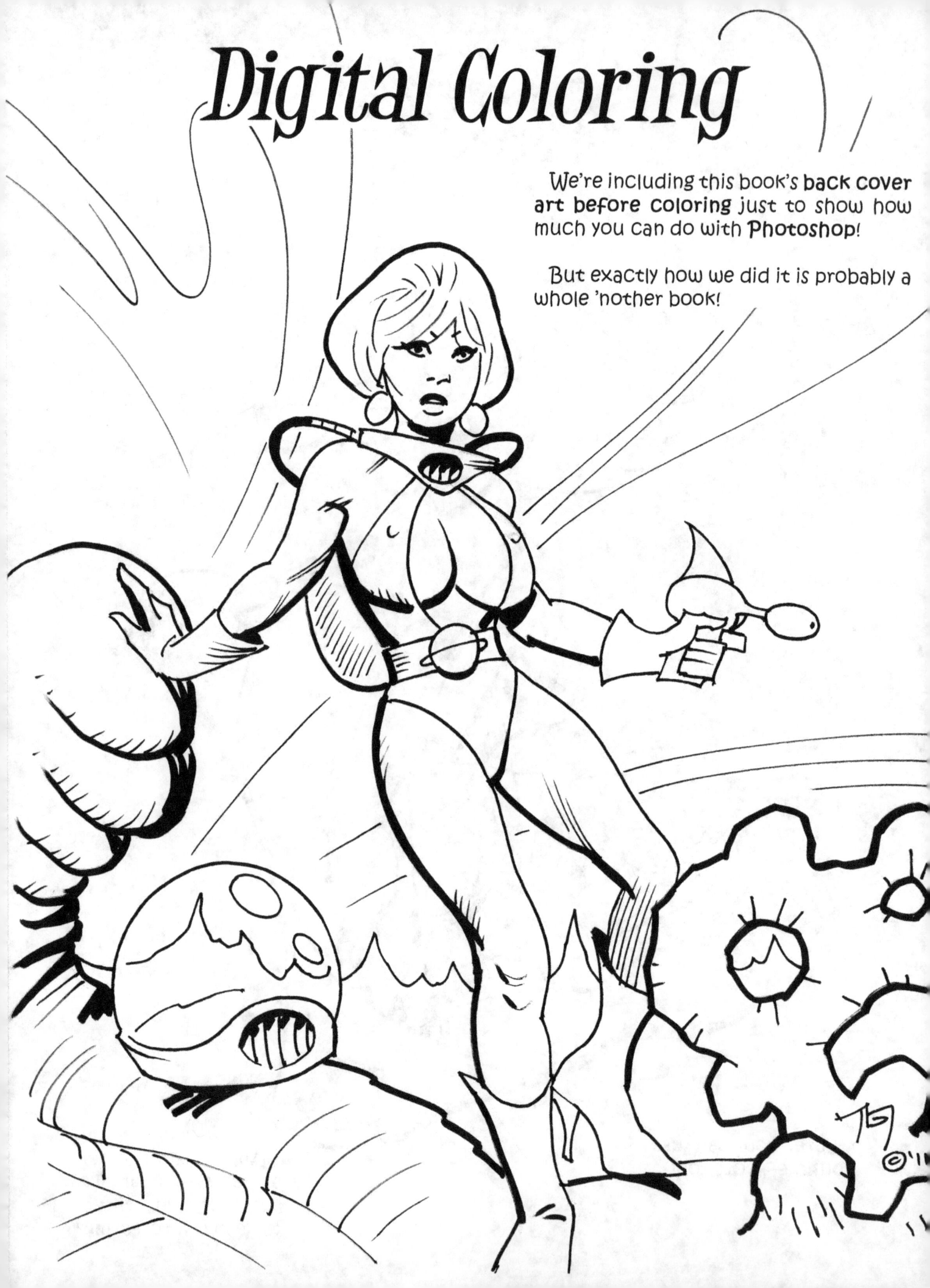

Hairstyles

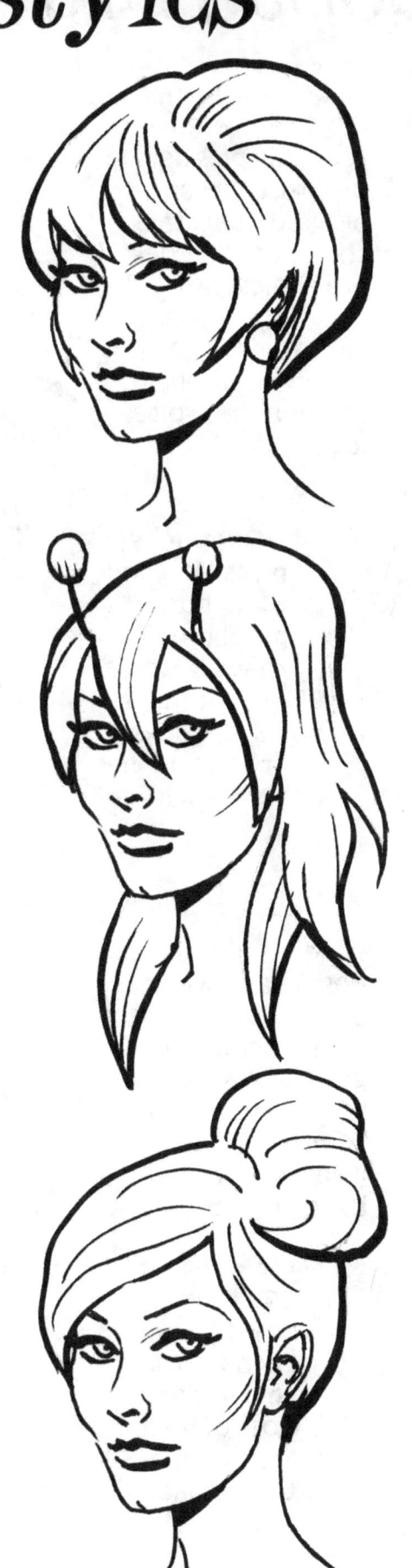
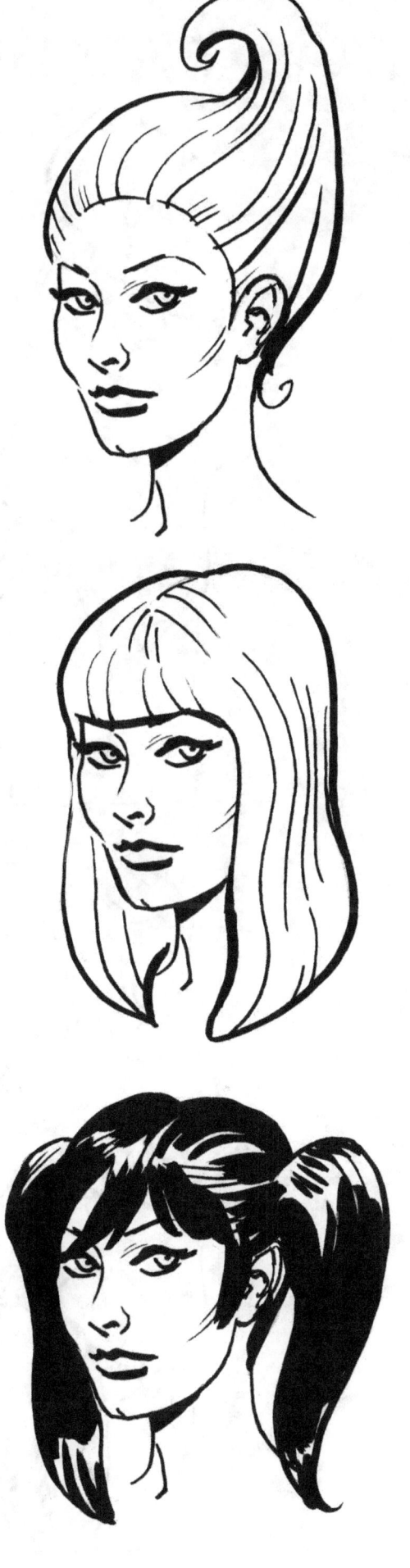

Space Girls like to look nice, just like girls every-where, so they spend a lot of **time** fixing up their **hair**!

Light years, in fact!

Some of these styles are **1960s**-inspired.

Some have **swoopy, swirly** shapes.

Others are "**classic**" and could be worn today!

You can easily create your **own** styles!

Just decide: **on** or **off** the face?

Costume

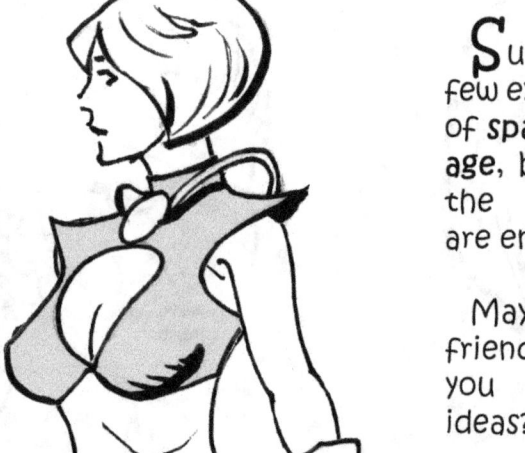

Sure, we got a few examples here of **space girl suit-age**, but naturally the possibilities are endless!

Maybe your girl-friend can help you with some ideas?

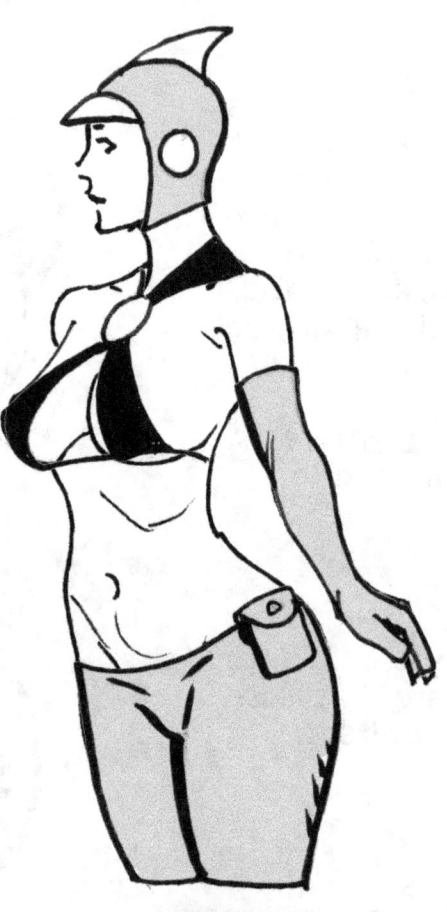

Completely **nude** is good too, but it's probably true that **some adornments** make things a little **more in-teresting!**

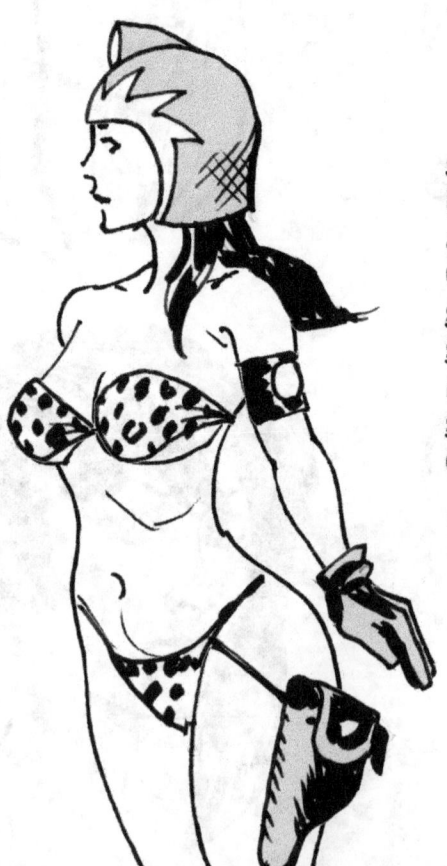

...And then in some **harsh** or **hostile situations,** a girl's gotta work with what she's **got,** so ya may get some **mix 'n' match** effects going on in true **castaway style!**

That could mean maybe some **animal skins** combined with **regula-tion** space gear!

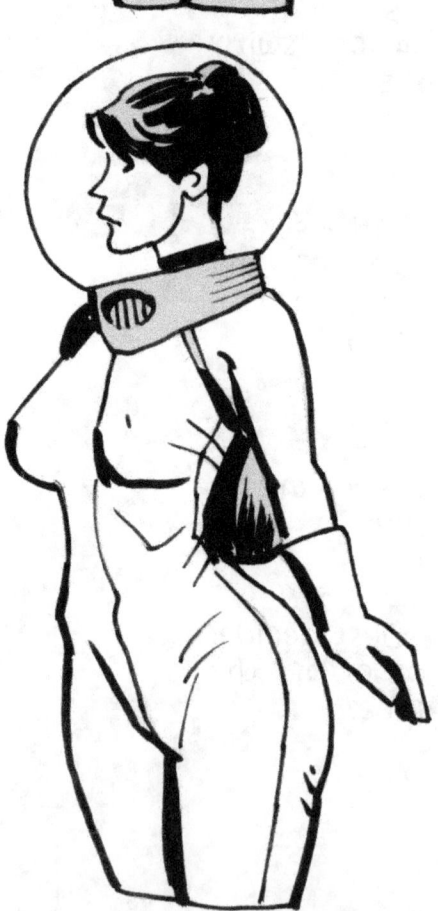

Making a Scene

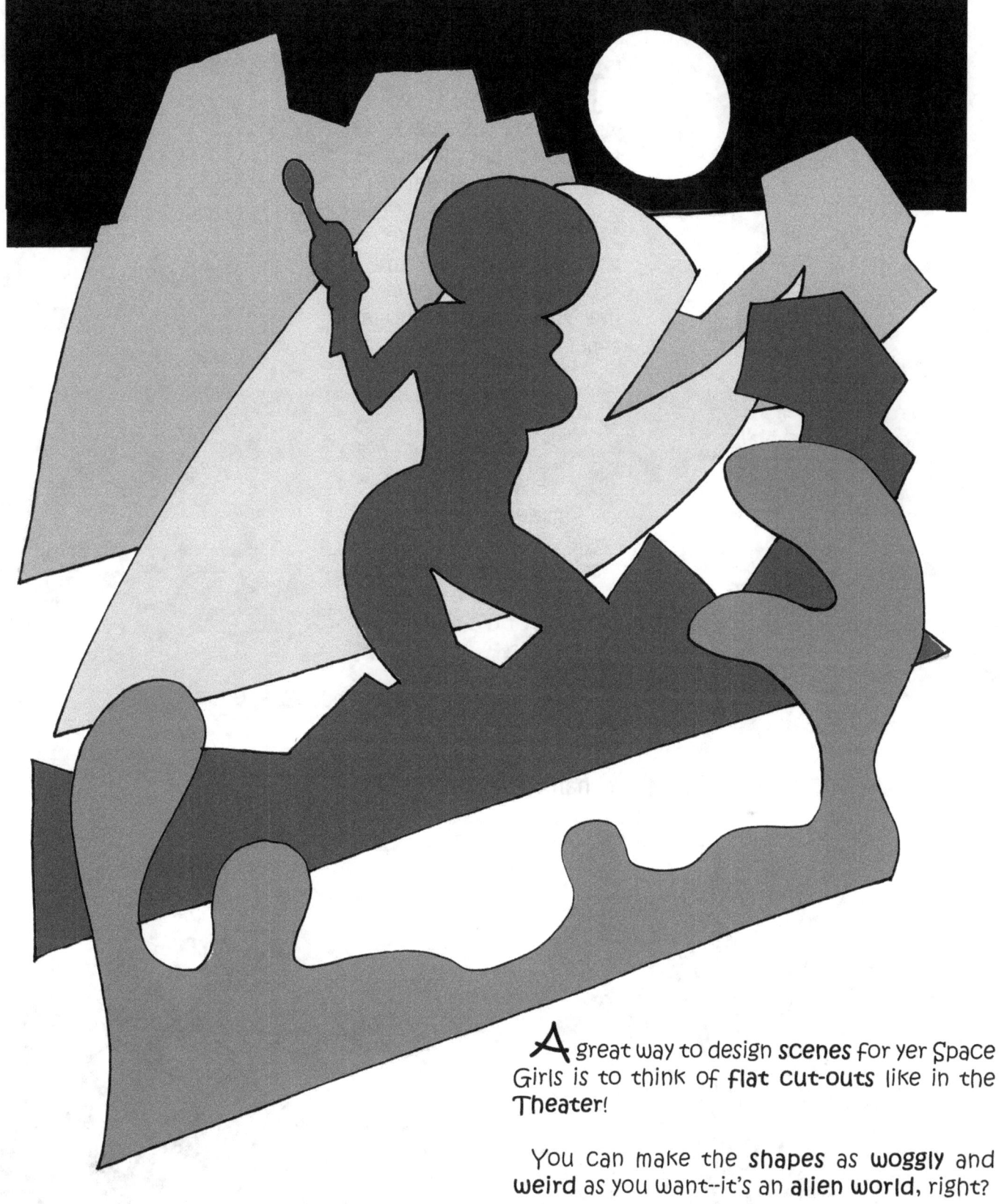

A great way to design **scenes** for yer Space Girls is to think of **flat cut-outs** like in the Theater!

You can make the **shapes** as **woggly** and **weird** as you want--it's an **alien world**, right?

This is sorta how old **3-D Comic Books** were made, too!

Alien Plant Life

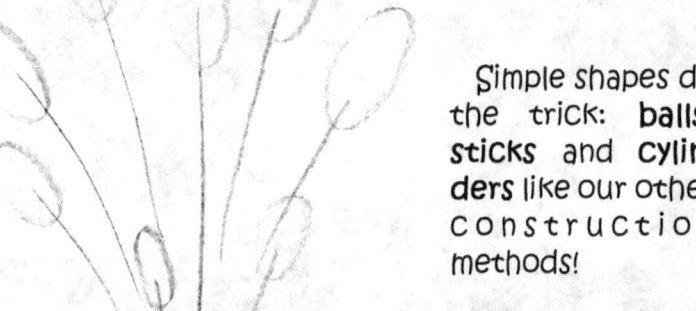

It's hard to go wrong here, as **every-thing** on other planets is sorta **weird already!**

And drawing these things is so much **fun** you'll wind up **inventing your own** in no time!

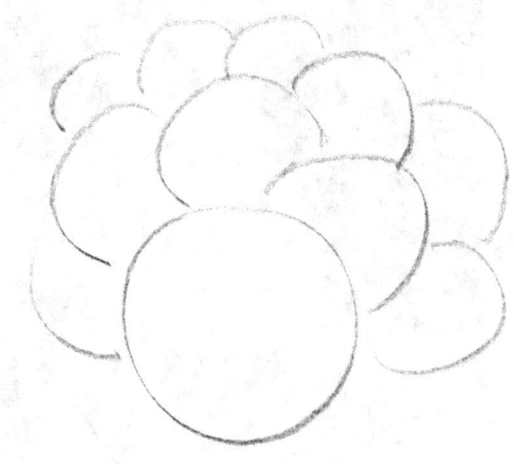

Simple shapes do the trick: **balls, sticks** and **cylinders** like our other c o n s t r u c t i o n methods!

Just remember **older growth** is gonna be **bigger** than the buds!

Use **shadows,** too!

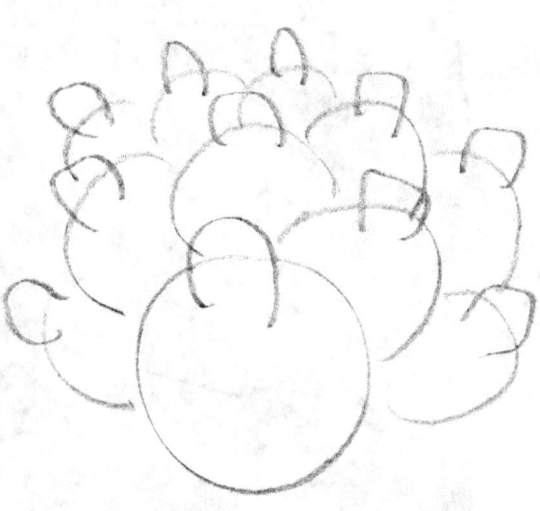

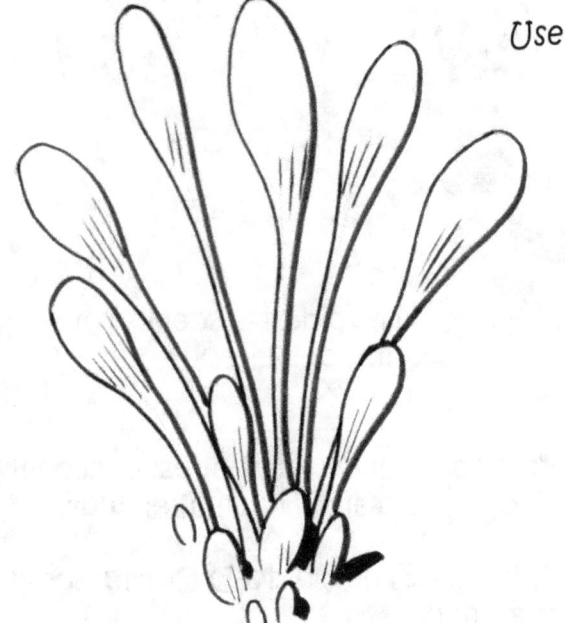

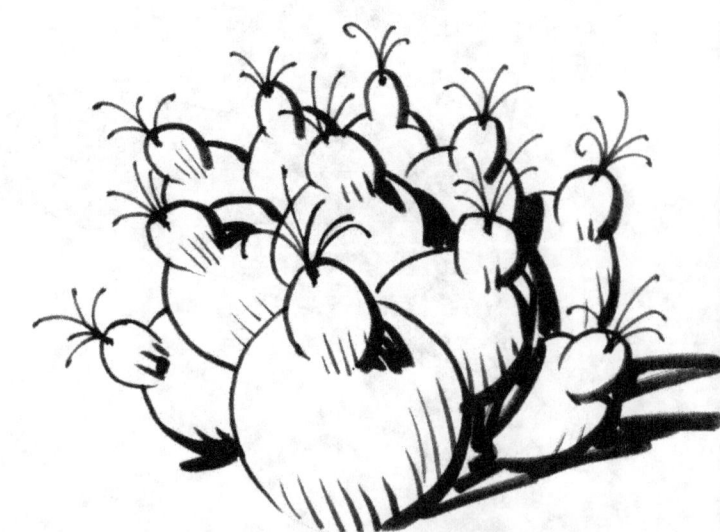

Good & Evil

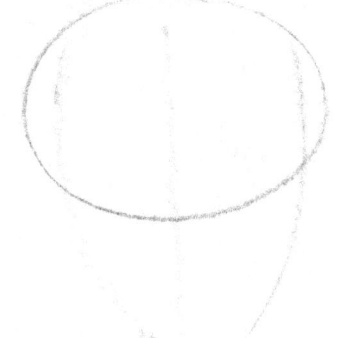

For some **head-on shots** use the **brain-case method** *first!*

Then drop in the **jaw line,** but **slice off** the **sides of the head!**

Ow!

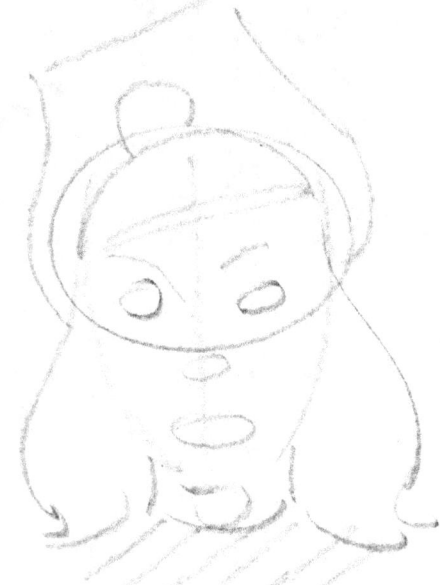

Adding simple features like **eyes, nose, mouth and hair** are further re-finements!

Any **costuming** you can indicate now too!

Keep everything minimal!

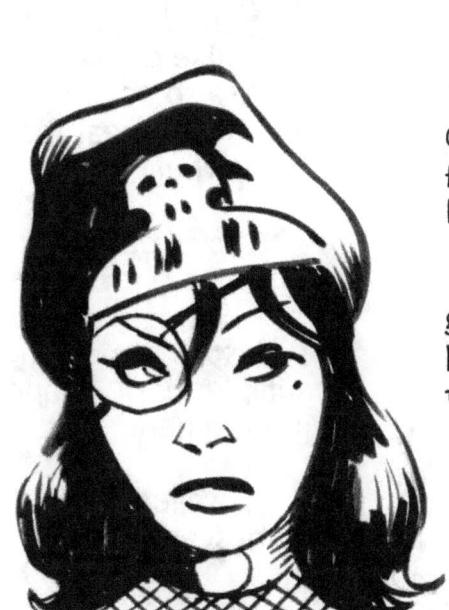

Your **Brush Pen** comes in handy for the **thick lines!**

Notice how we got some good **blacks** even on the blonde girl?

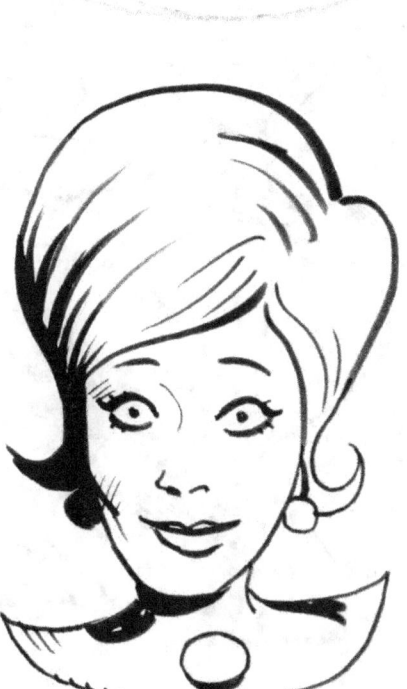

Alien Monsters

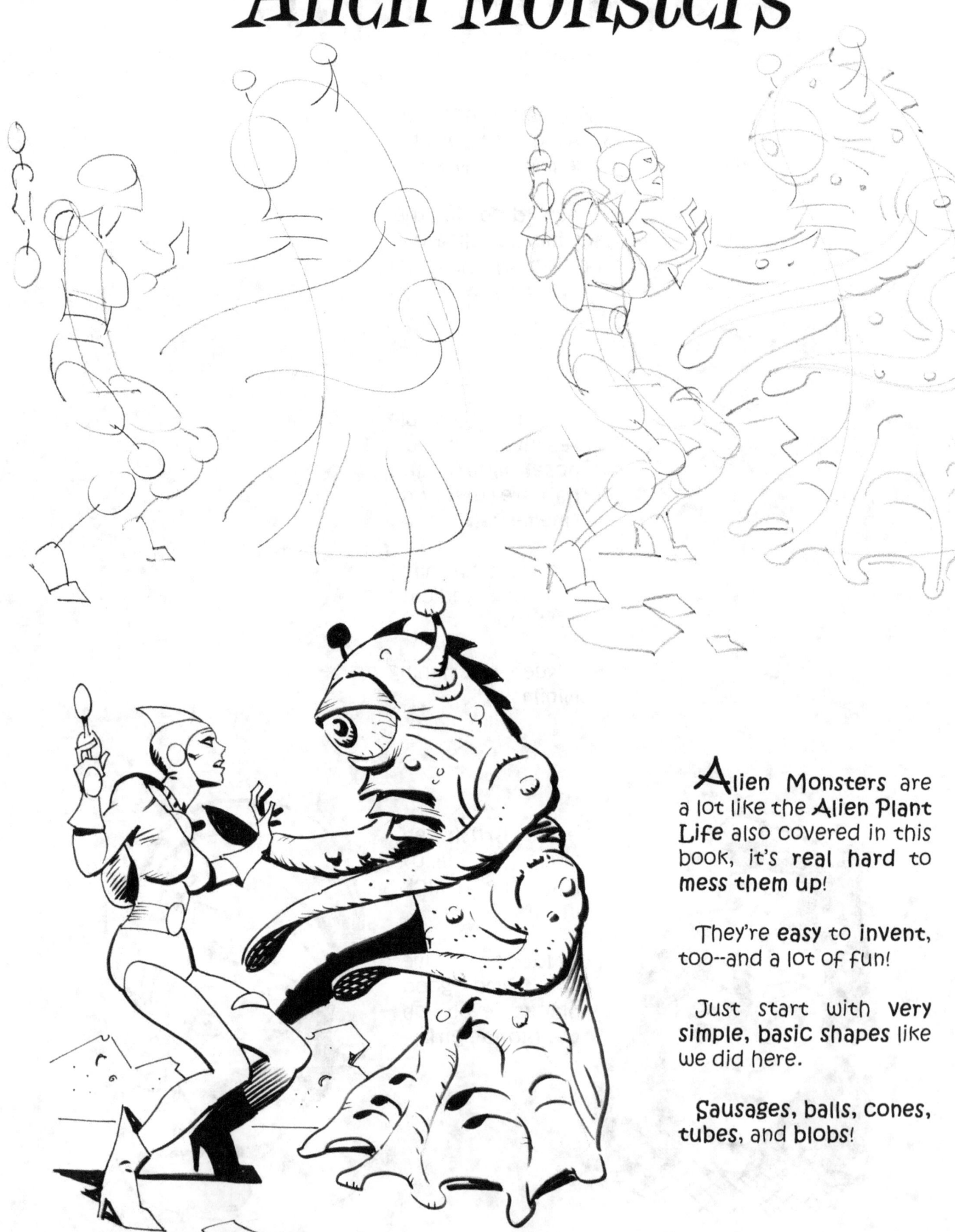

Alien Monsters are a lot like the **Alien Plant Life** also covered in this book, it's real hard to **mess them up!**

They're **easy** to **invent**, too--and a lot of fun!

Just start with **very simple, basic shapes** like we did here.

Sausages, balls, cones, tubes, and blobs!

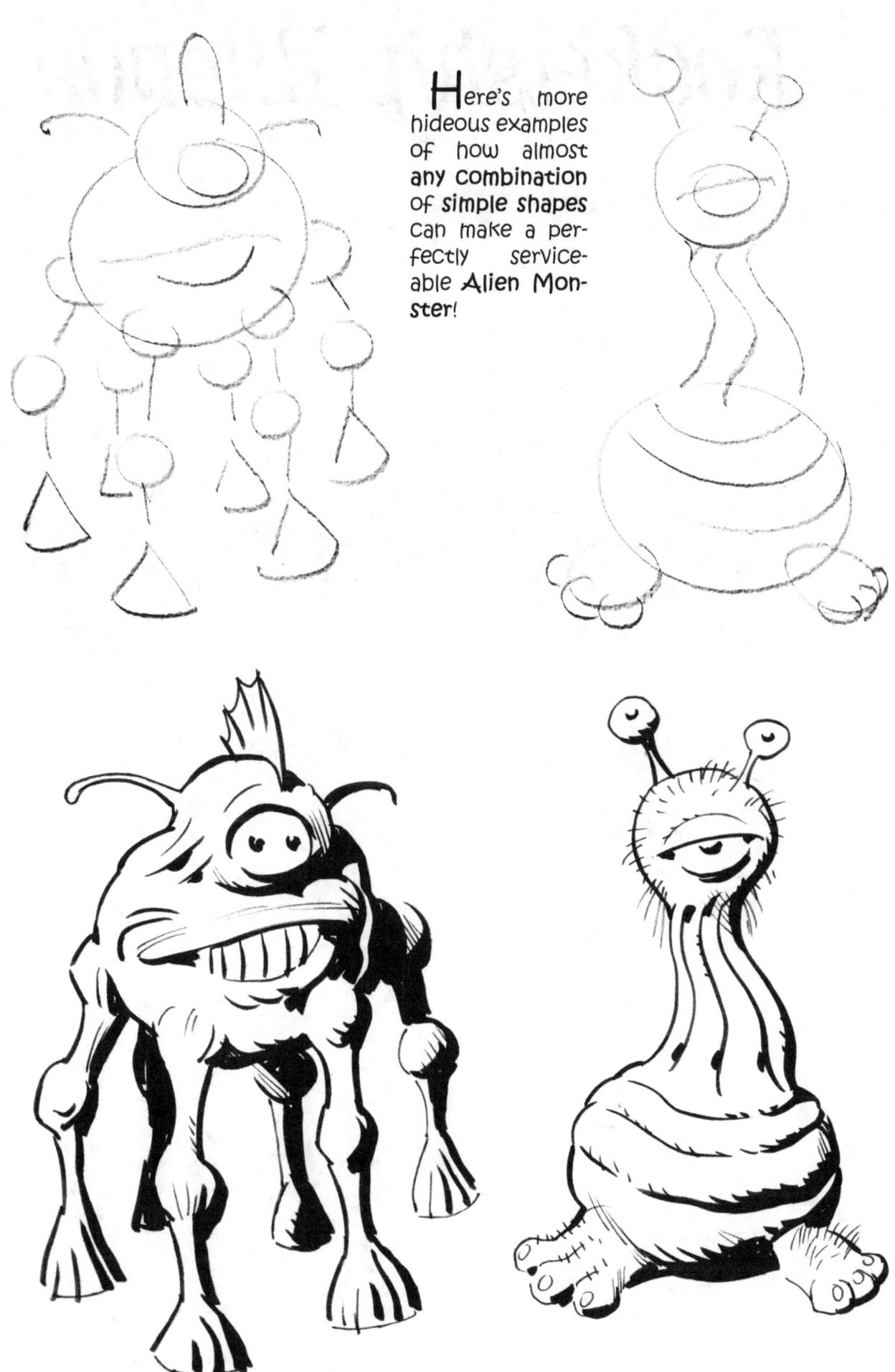

Here's more hideous examples of how almost any combination of simple shapes can make a perfectly serviceable Alien Monster!

Rocketship Rhonda

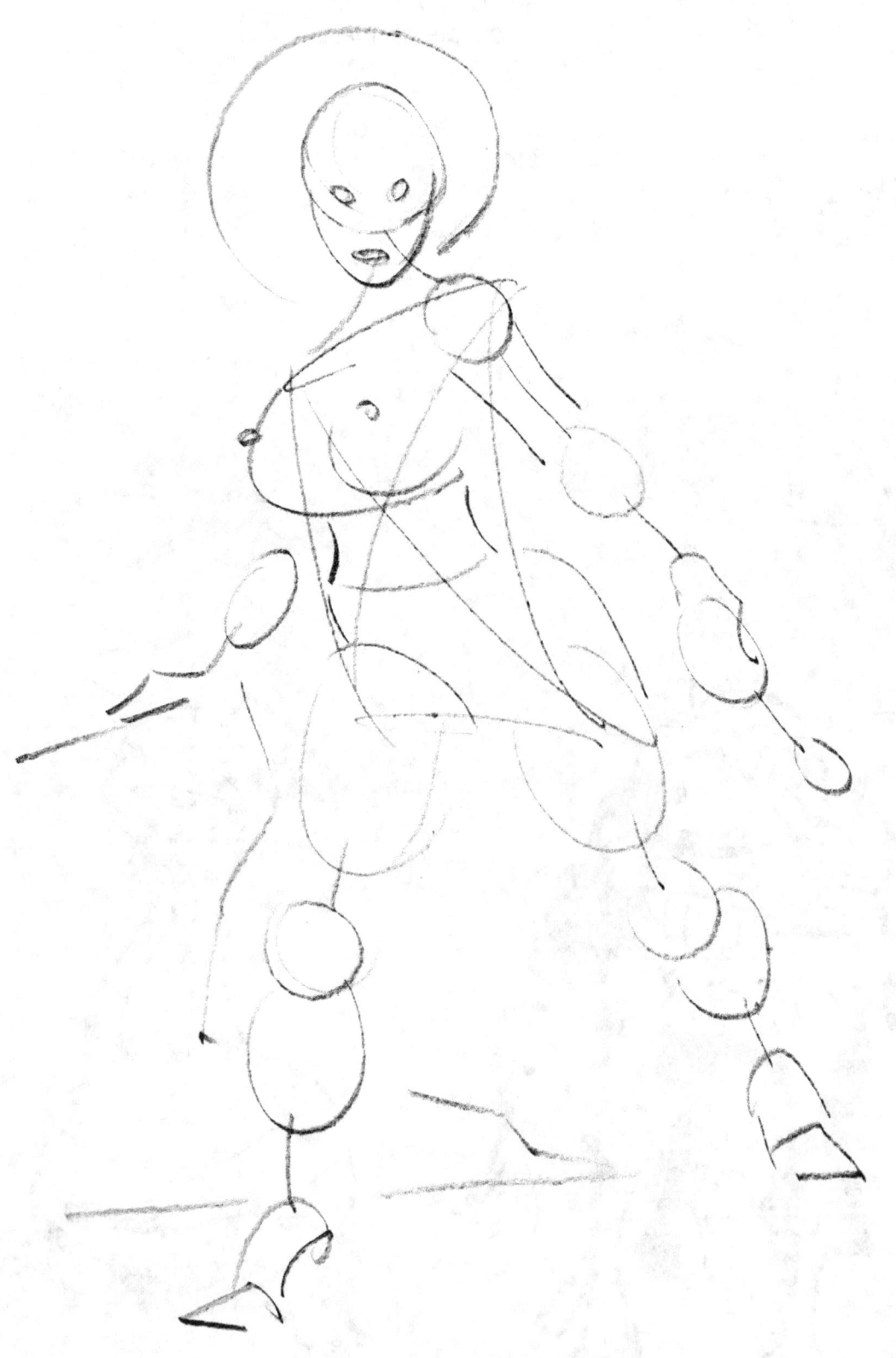

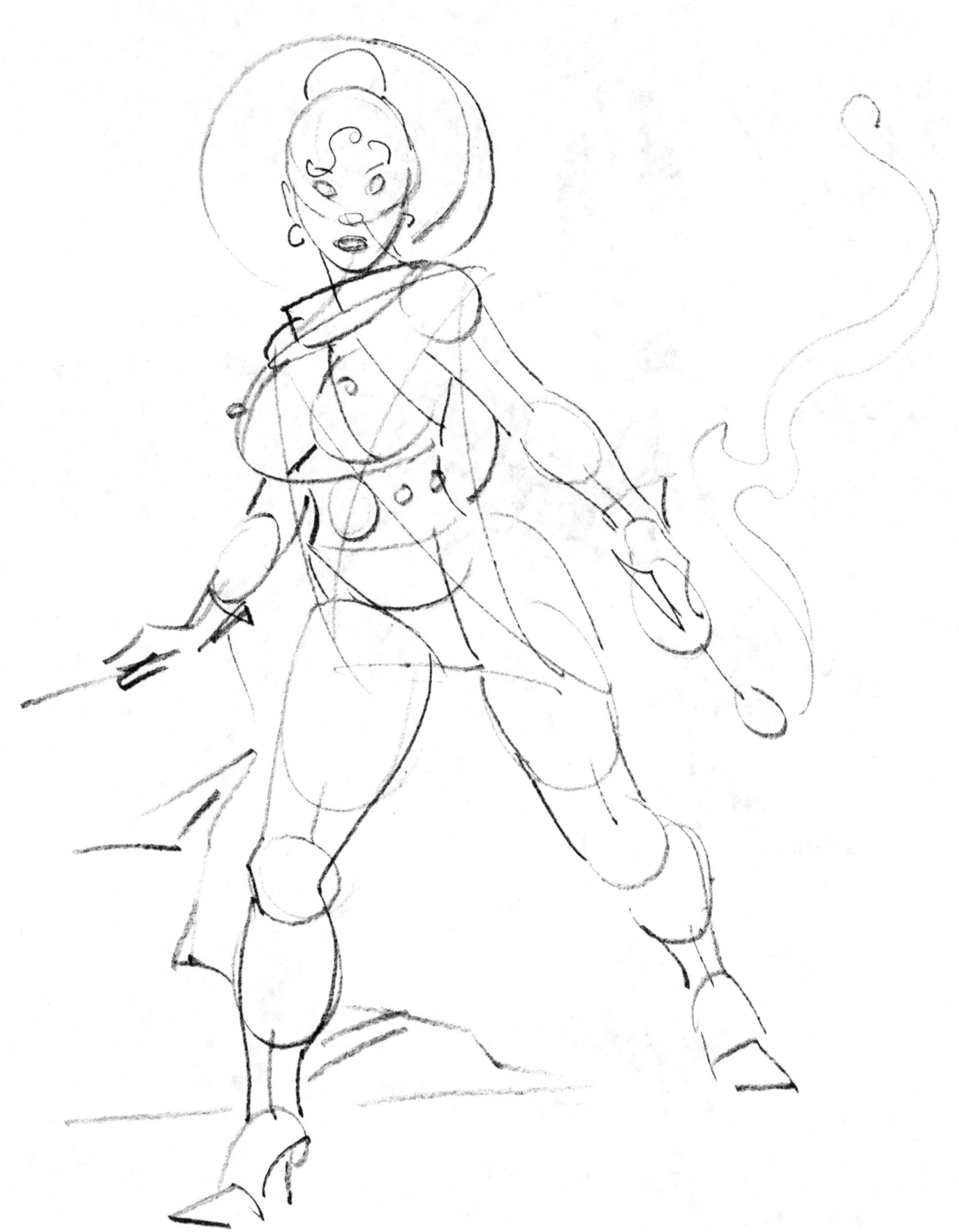

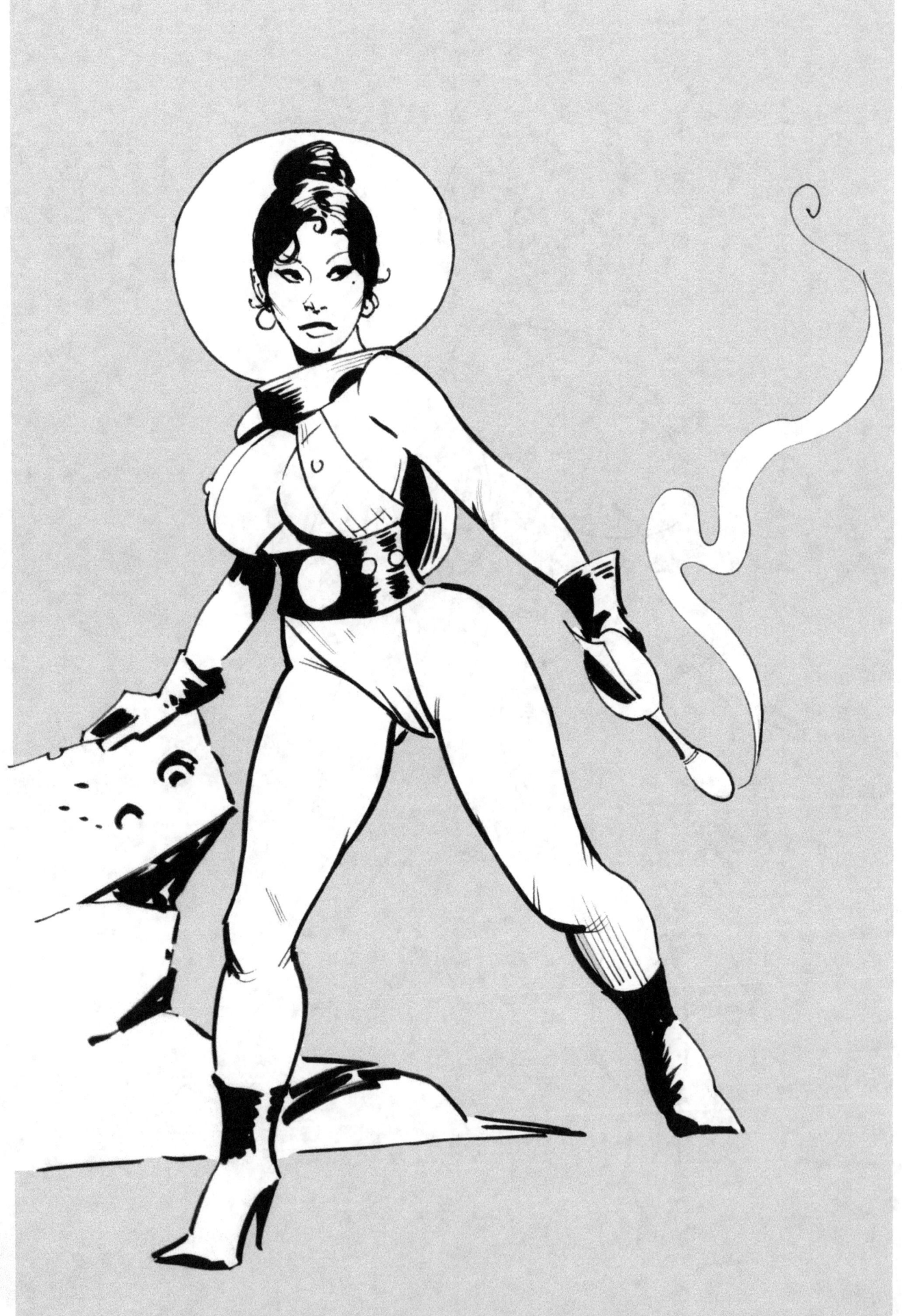

Ursula Orion

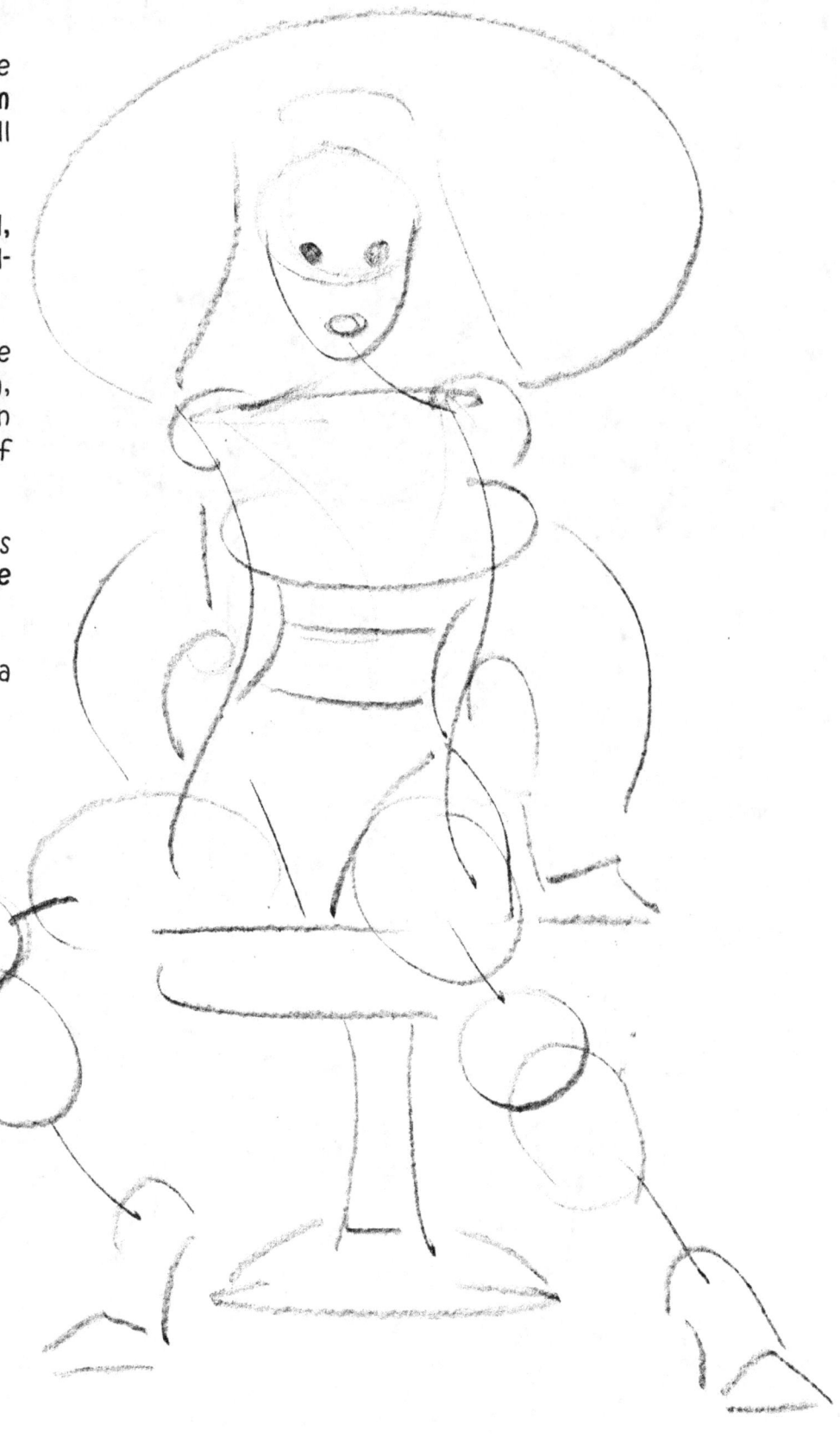

Still the same simple little system we've been doing all along!

The **Playing Card**, **Lollipops**, **circles**, **cylinders** and **ovals**!

Be careful where you **put them**, though--that's when you **commit** yourself to a pose!

Notice that this time we **twisted the card side-to-side**?

Ya can't **do** with a **real** Card!

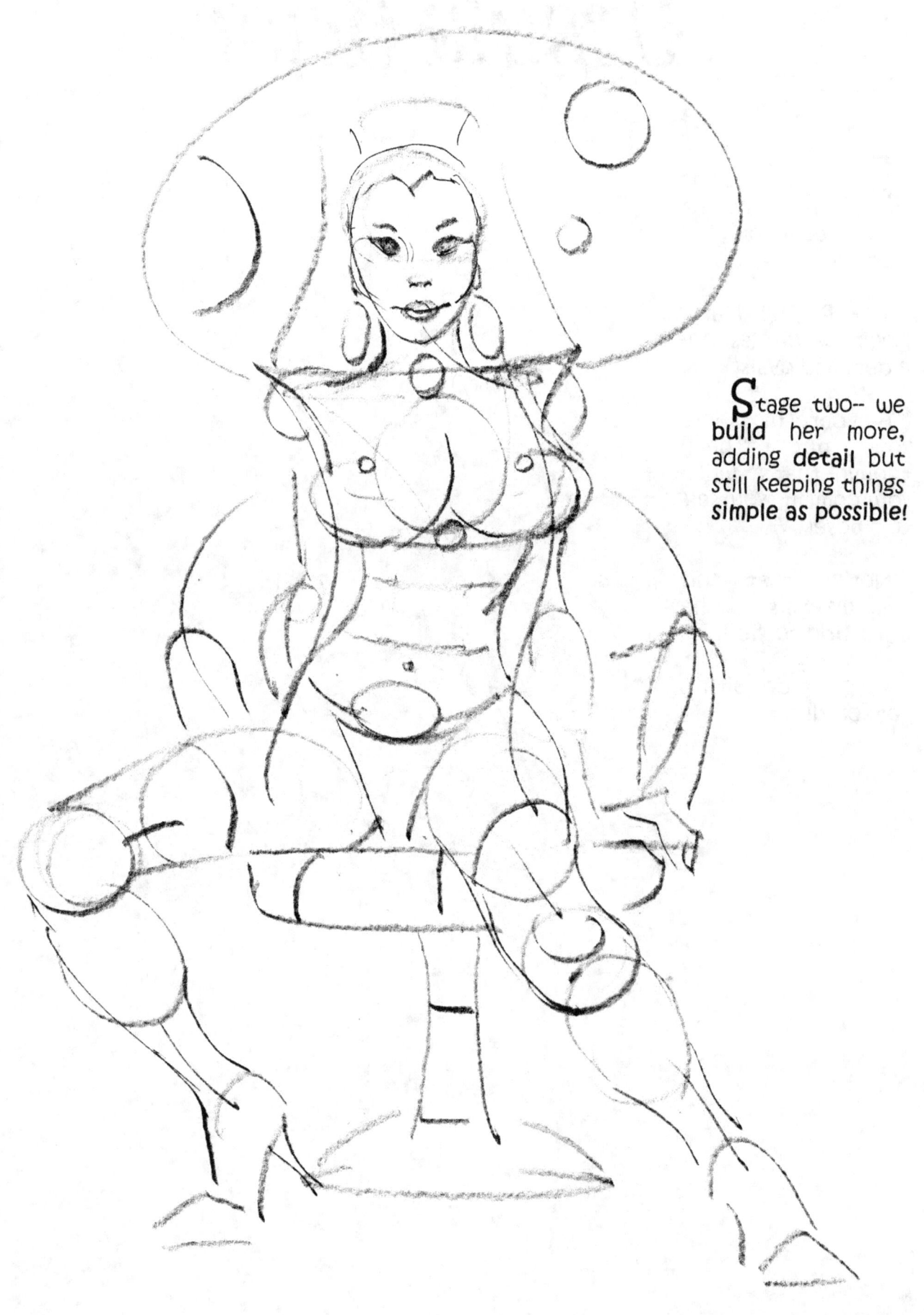

Stage two-- we **build** her more, adding **detail** but still keeping things simple as possible!

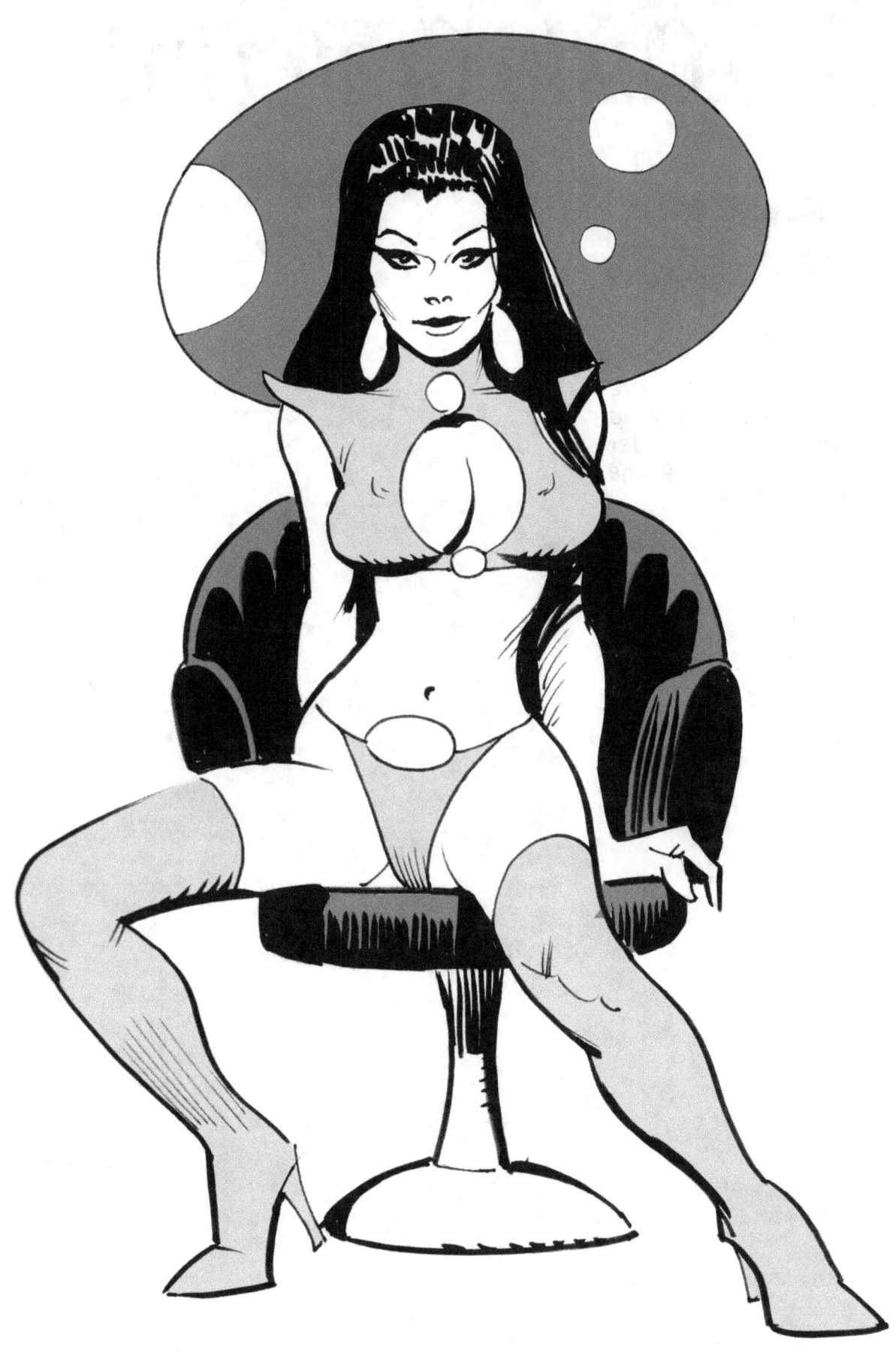

Carla Craterini

Balance is impor-
tant, you don't want
your girls **tipping over**!

Or **do ya**?

Anyway, make sure
the **feet** are planted
pretty good **under
where most of the
weight is**!

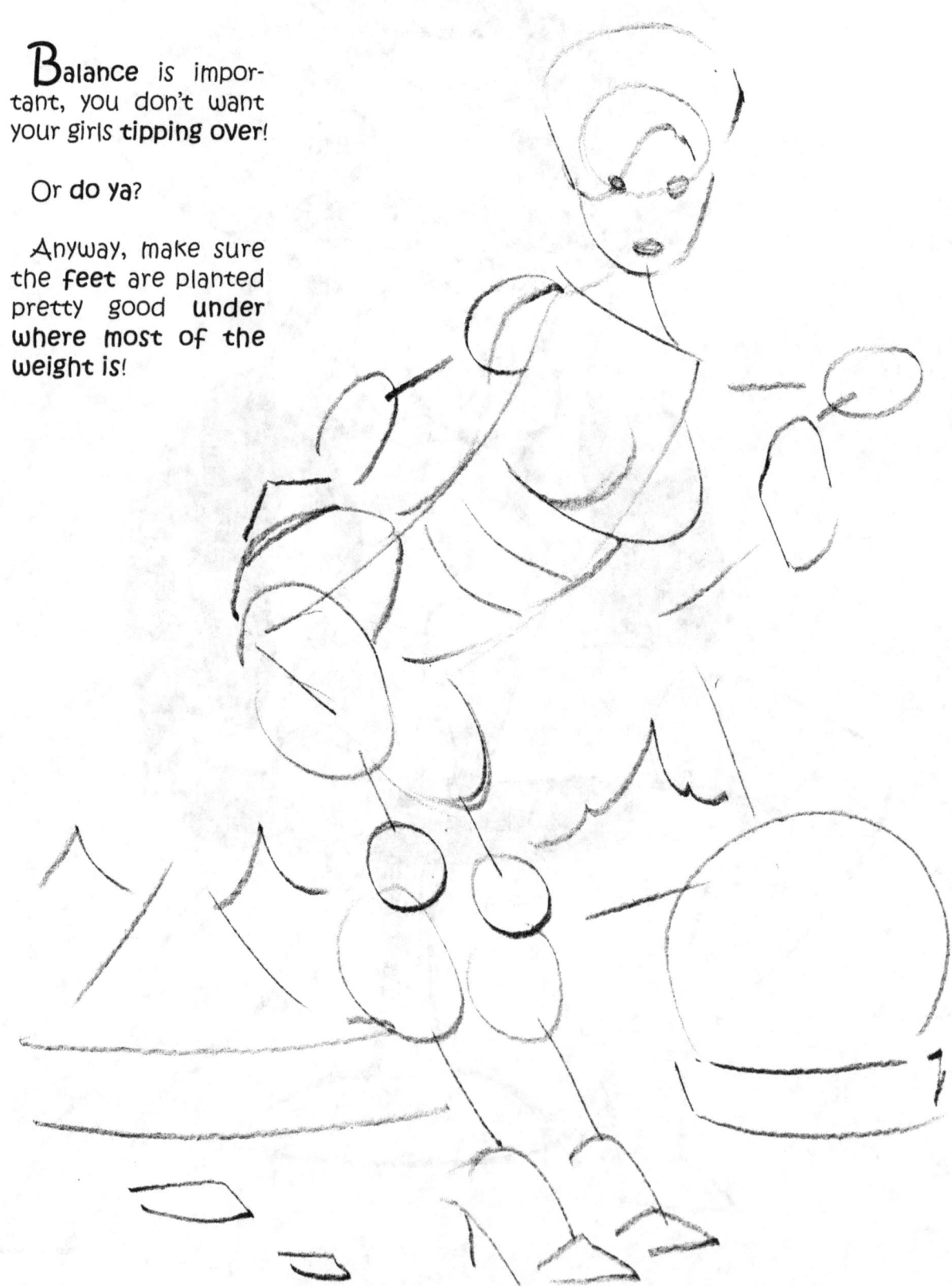

You can see all the **extra stuff** we stuck in, heck we got excited!

Even that **spaceship** circling out there is hoping for an **easy pickup**, which is pretty **easy** in **zero gravity**.

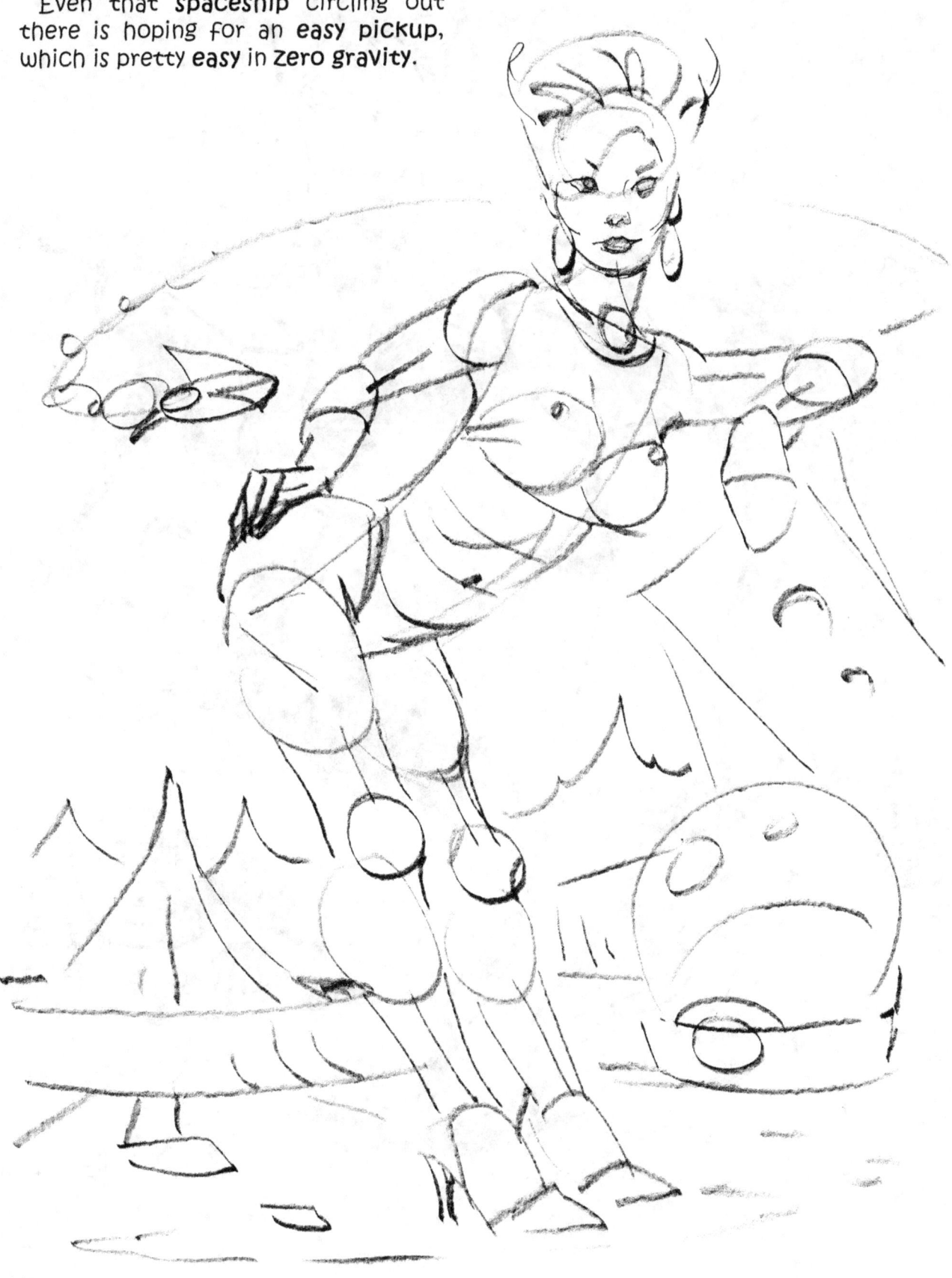

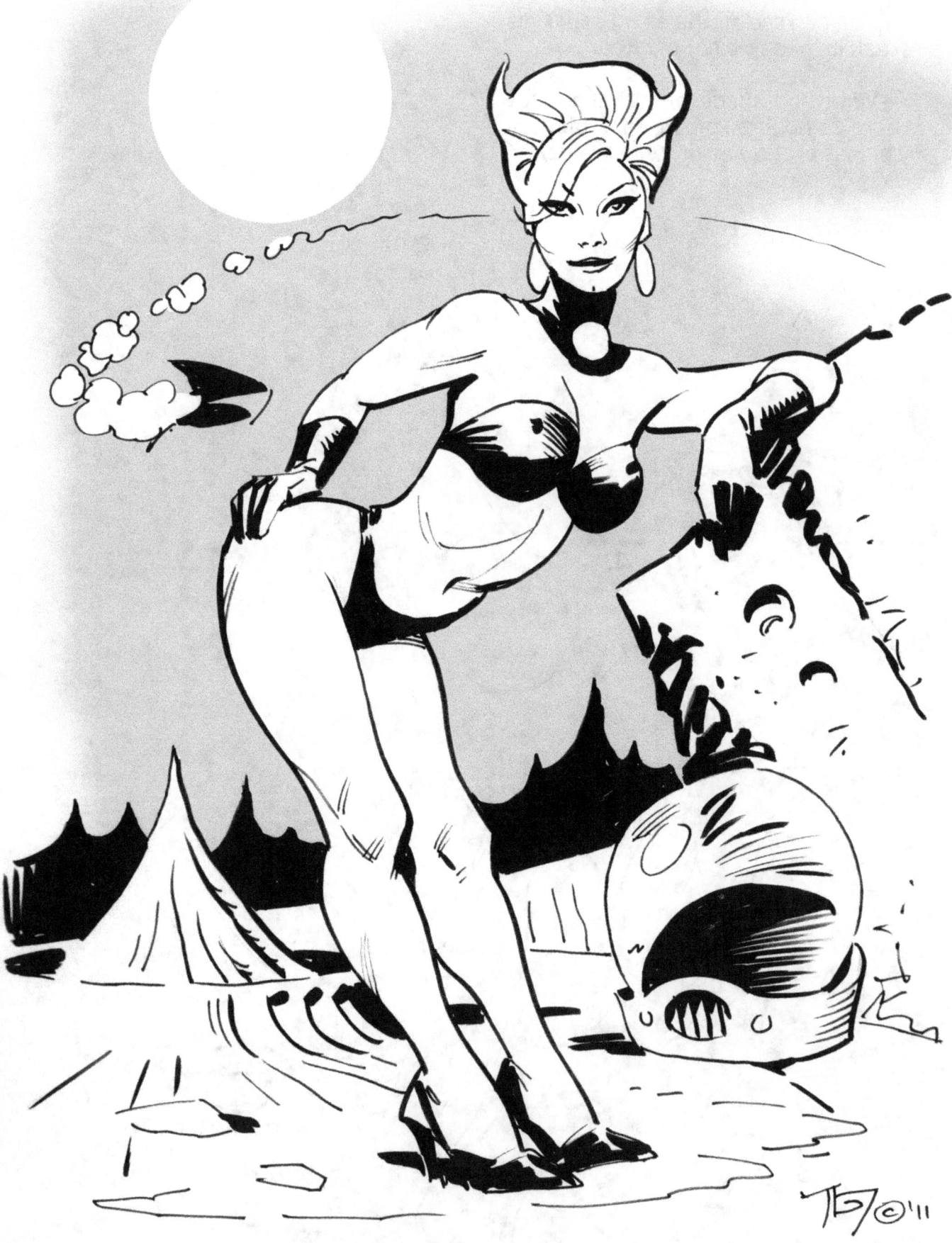

Starry-Eyed Stella

She's all star-struck, wishin' upon a star, you get the picture...

Notice how in the drawing at left the **Playing Card** is still the **basis** and **foundation** of the whole pose!

You can invent your own **new poses** all day long with this technique, just draw the card at some **new angle** and then **build on it**!

The **key** to drawing **good rocks** is to make 'em look **solid** and **3-D**!

We outlined 'em **first** here, then divided **them** up into **planes** like a **crystal** or **diamond**.

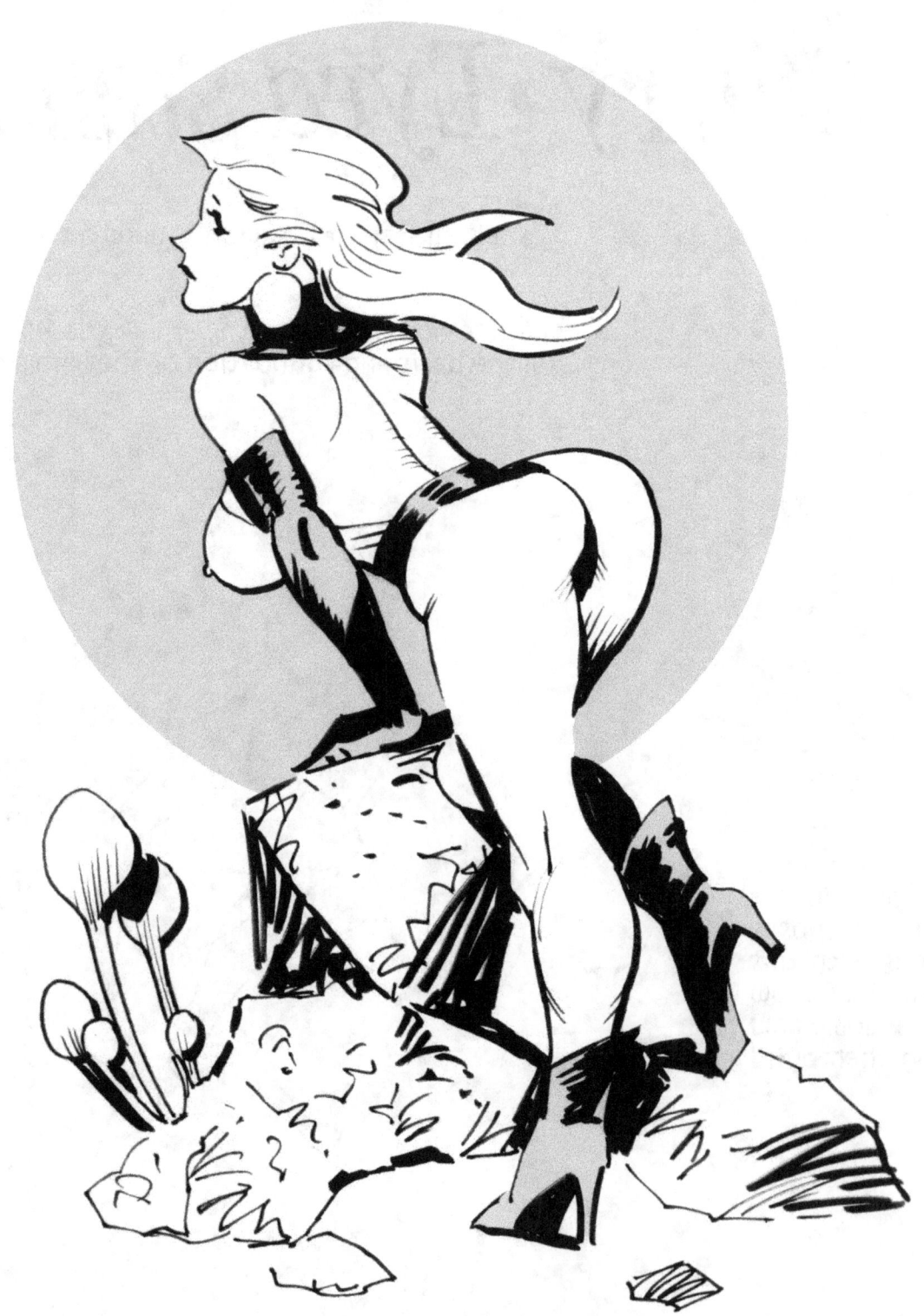

Here's **Stella** all inked-up and ready to rocket outta there!

Notice how we added a spot of **Alien Plant** life? That helps **balance-out** the composition!

We also "broke-up" a lot of the **planes and angles** on the **rocks** so they still look sorta **solid** but not so **geometrical**!

GOOD LUCK AND HAPPY DRAWING, SPACEMAN!